# SKILL IN SPORT

# SKILL IN SPORT

## The Attainment of Proficiency

by

## B. KNAPP

*M.Com.*

LONDON
ROUTLEDGE & KEGAN PAUL

*First published 1963*
*by Routledge & Kegan Paul Limited*
*Broadway House, 68–74 Carter Lane*
*London, E.C.4*

*Printed Offset Litho in Great Britain*
*by Cox & Wyman Ltd.*
*London, Fakenham and Reading*

*Second impression 1964*
*Third impression 1966*
*Fourth impression 1967*
*Fifth impression 1970*

*SBN 7100 1691 3*

TO MY MOTHER

# CONTENTS

vii

# Contents

# ILLUSTRATIONS

## FIGURES

## PLATES

*(Between pages 100 and 101)*

# PREFACE

THIS BOOK has been written primarily for teachers, coaches and sportsmen though it is hoped that anyone interested in acquiring skill in recreational physical activities may find it of value. It is concerned with skill in activities in the gymnasium, on the playing fields, in the swimming bath and the great outdoors. The need for such a book was first realized when I was asked for reading material after giving a lecture on the acquisition of skill at a Summer School held at a specialist college of Physical Education.

In lecturing to undergraduates studying Physical Education as a subject for a degree I found that they preferred to deal with the more practical issues first and be led gradually into a consideration of the more theoretical aspects of the subject. Their preference has determined the arrangement of this book. Readers who would prefer a more logical development of the subject should read Chapters VII, VIII, and IX after Chapter I.

The material for this book has been collected from many sources and has been checked against my own practical experience both in learning physical skills and in teaching them. The evidence, some of which has been printed in smaller type so that readers may omit it if they wish, is of several kinds and the reader must weigh it accordingly. First there are the results from stringent psychological experiments. The difficulty here is that much of the work has been concerned with verbal and fine motor skills and findings in this field may not be applicable to activities involving the big-muscle groups of the body. Then there are the results from the relatively small amount of research into the acquisition of gross motor skills carried out mainly in America by physical educationists and published for the most part in the Research Quarterly to which acknowledgment is now made. Many of these experiments have been conducted on relatively few subjects and it is therefore difficult to make general deductions from them with certainty. Lastly there are observations made by various authorities in the field of sport and physical education. Since these are subjective in nature they must obviously be accepted with some reservations.

This book therefore claims to be only an interim statement based on my interpretation and evaluation of the evidence and I shall be pleased to receive comments, criticisms and data which may throw further light on the subject of skill acquisition in activities in physical education and physical recreation.

Even when the best methods for acquiring skill in any activity are known with certainty there will still be an art in applying them so that any particular individual may benefit. I appreciate also that there will be many occasions when the objective of acquiring skill will be subordinate to other aims and that on these occasions the best methods for acquiring skill may have to be sacrificed. I hope, however, that this book will give a sound basis on which to build a more complete knowledge of the subject, will stimulate discussion and more precise observation and will provide initial references and encouragement for the further research which is so acutely needed in this field.

My thanks are due to the University of Birmingham for granting me three months' study leave and to Mr. A. D. Munrow, Director of the Department of Physical Education and to my colleagues who made it possible for me to take advantage of it. I am grateful to the many persons – psychologists, physical educationists and others – who have given me advice and encouragement. I am particularly indebted to Mr. A. T. Welford and Professor P. Meredith for the valuable discussions I had with them and for their interest in this project, and to Dr. A. L. Haigh for his comments on Chapter VII. I must especially thank Mr. P. C. McIntosh for reading the whole typescript and making many valuable comments and criticisms, and for his continuous encouragement.

# I

## SKILL DEFINED

IN EVERYDAY SPEECH the term skill is used in many different ways. Parents talk about their children having just acquired the skill of walking, of swimming or of kicking a football. Industry classifies men into the skilled, semi-skilled and unskilled. The journalist writes about the skill of Stanley Matthews, Johnny Haynes and Jimmy Greaves and the lack of skill of many other professional footballers. The physical educationist teaches gymnastic skills. People talk of the skill of the doctor, the farmer, the athletic coach and the mathematician. Indeed it has been said that 'if we give the term its widest possible meaning, almost every activity of a living creature is essentially an act of skill'.[1]

It is necessary however for the purposes of this book to try to be more precise. Although rote memorization and verbal reasoning are skills they are mainly mental and will therefore be excluded from consideration. This does not imply that motor skills do not involve mental as well as physical activity but only that the overt actions form an essential part. Indeed there is a tendency for the physical educationist to pay too much attention to the motor aspect of skill because in activities involving the big-muscle groups the movement part is the most obvious. It must however be remembered that all skills are sensori-motor and that the information from the sensory organs and the directions from the brain are as important to skill as the motor aspect.

The perceptual-motor skills can be divided into those involving mainly the big-muscle groups and those where the size of movements is usually small and the activity is concentrated in the limbs or other small musculatures. The latter include activities such as drawing, typing, and operating or assembling many industrial machines. The former include athletic activities of all kinds. But the division is not clear-cut, for skills involving mainly fine motor co-ordinations also involve the trunk muscles to a considerable degree either in maintaining relatively stationary postures or of orienting the limbs towards the work area such as a desk, bench or machine. Similarly most gross motor skills also involve some use of fine motor co-ordinations. The distinction is useful to a certain extent because in fine motor co-ordinations the factor of strength is usually secondary to speed or precision or both whereas in many gross motor acts strength is very important.

In physical education and physical recreation the main concern is with skills involving the active use of big-muscle groups but fine motor co-ordinations are often also involved. The skills differ one from another in the contribution of the various factors in producing the skilled man. Sometimes strength is of major importance; at other times speed or accuracy or timing or the appreciation of the needs of the situation.

The term 'a skill' can be used in physical education in many different ways and some examples are as follows:

1. It may refer to an act which arises largely through maturation such as walking, running, hopping, curling, stretching, twisting and other acts of this kind in their more elementary stages. These acts have also been called activities, fundamental skills and basic skills. Since skill is learned and these acts are largely unlearned it would be best not to use the term skill but to call these basic movements. Practice of these basic movements which do not have a clearly defined goal keeps them in action and ready to be called on when needed. When however they are practised with a specific end in view as in race-walking or the hop, step and jump then they move into the third group of examples below.

2. 'A skill' may refer to an act in which the aim is the production of some pattern of movements which is considered to be technically sound. Thus an individual may be able to carry out the Western Roll but only over a low height. A shot-putter may have a mechanically efficient style and yet be able to putt the

shot only a short distance. A ballet dancer may be able to do certain steps with technical perfection and yet not capture the spirit of the dance. A tennis player may be able to produce a mechanically sound forehand drive when practising but not when playing a match. It would be better to reserve the term technique to apply to this aspect of skill. Technique may then be defined as that pattern of movement which is technically sound for the particular skill and which is an integral part but not the whole part of that skill.

3. 'A skill' may refer to an act or a whole collection of actions in which there is a clearly defined goal or set of goals. It will then include on the one hand skills like javelin throwing, diving and vaulting in which the technique plays the major part and on the other, the skill of playing football or hockey in which the reactions to the external environment become vital. The hockey player may have excellent stickwork but unless he can use it to advantage in the game he has not learned the skill of playing hockey. The tennis player may have highly efficient techniques but may lack skill in tennis because he does not perceive the right moment to use those techniques. A skilled footballer or any other games player must take action which is appropriate and therefore the skill involves interpreting the needs of the situation and making the right decision as well as carrying out the necessary movements. In games, decision-making is a vital part of the skill.

This matter will be considered again in Chapter VIII but for the moment it is necessary to point out that in many skills, such as shot-putting, vaulting and swimming, the crucial factor is that of the motor action whereas in team games the perception of what is happening around the individual and of the necessary response to the situation is extremely important. The varying contribution of the external requirements of any skill will have an effect on acquisition and on the suitability of particular methods of learning.

The skill of playing a game, rowing a race, boxing or fencing in a match, involves not only the actions taken at any one time but also the actions taken over the whole period of the activity on that occasion. Tactics and strategy therefore also form an important part of these and similar skills.

A skill is any definable activity in which 'skill' can be

shown. A skill can be performed with a great deal of skill or with little skill. It is necessary then to try to define the term skill when used without a definite or indefinite article. This is not easy for in much of the literature on skill no definition is given. The definition which it is proposed to use in this book is a modification of that given by Guthrie.[2] It is that skill is the learned ability to bring about predetermined results with maximum certainty, often with the minimum outlay of time or energy or both. Thus in the case of any gymnastic vault it is the ability to perform the vault satisfactorily on any and every occasion which would make us call that person a skilled performer of the particular vault. In this case the outlay of energy is only of importance if the individual has to do a programme of vaults as he might have to do if taking part in a gymnastic competition. In lawn tennis however two individuals may be equally skilled so far as the certainty with which they hit and place the ball is concerned. But the one who expends least energy for the same results will have the advantage and will therefore be the more skilled. In industry on the other hand the most skilled person is often the one who has the ability to bring about a predetermined end result over and over again at great speed. In other words here it is important for there to be a minimum outlay of both time and energy.

The predetermined results may be in terms of speed, precision, power, quality, difficulty or any combination of these. Diving and figure-skating for instance involve a combination of precision, difficulty and quality. The predetermined result may on the other hand be in terms of winning as in games and many sports. In this case individuals may achieve the same end result in many different ways. In this case individuals could use entirely different patterns of movement to deal adequately with similar situations.

This definition that skill is the learned ability to bring about predetermined results with maximum certainty, often with the minimum outlay of time or energy or both, implies that in the complex skills of physical education and physical recreation a person can only be more, or less, skilful. Perfection is not attainable. But at what point should it be said that an individual is skilled in an activity or has learned some specific skill? This must be an arbitrary decision in each case but should, accord-

4

ing to the definition, depend on how closely or with what certainty the goal is achieved. Frequently, however, skill is judged by the character of the movement itself rather than by the results achieved. This is only satisfactory if there is in fact a close relationship between the character of the movement and the actual results. In activities where technique is important, the smooth, relaxed and graceful movements which some people correlate with skill are frequently the sign of good co-ordination and therefore are connected with good results. But skill in general cannot be judged in terms of the movement patterns for in mental skills the overt actions are relatively insignificant. In many physical skills, as has already been pointed out, the interpretation of the needs of the situation and the making of decisions is important. There may well be certain general qualities of skilled performance such as timing but until these can be more clearly recognized it would seem better not to use them to define skill.

The definition has stated that skill is learned, but not all learning produces skill, for inefficient actions may be learned and also movements which do not bring about the predetermined result. Some non-swimmers have learned just such movements which make the acquisition of the skill of swimming that much more difficult. Skill, although not co-extensive with learning, yet involves and implies learning.

Learning has been defined as 'the internal neural process assumed to occur whenever a change in performance, not due to growth or fatigue, exhibits itself'.[3] A child grows and his growth may affect his performance but this is not learning. A person may develop strength or endurance and thereby cause changes in his performance, but this is not learning. The performance of an old person may deteriorate through age or that of an individual through injury to an eye or other sensory organ, but this is not learning. A person's performance may change because of fatigue or emotion or alcohol or the surrounding conditions, but in so far as any such change is temporary it is not learning. Learning may then be considered to be a more or less permanent change in performance associated with experience but excluding changes which occur through maturation and degeneration, or through alterations in the receptor or effector organs.

Changes such as increases in strength and endurance which occur in the effector mechanisms through practice are not therefore part of skill though they affect the performance of a skill and its results. Skill may contribute to an activity and yet not be the whole of that activity. There are other factors besides skill which may affect performance in a skill. Although reference will be made to many skills and to factors other than skill which determine the speed with which a given level of performance is reached, this book is mainly concerned with the acquisition of skill and the contribution of skill to skills.

# II

## CURVES OF LEARNING

PHYSICAL SKILLS cannot be learned without 'having a go' and few can be acquired at a single trial. The skills involved in physical education and physical recreation are usually complex and require many repetitions and considerable time. If performance is measured in some way the measurements may be plotted on a graph against the amount of practice. There will be considerable variation from period to period but the trend, which is shown by the general shape of the curve, is called a curve of learning. Although these learning curves vary from individual to individual, from activity to activity and according

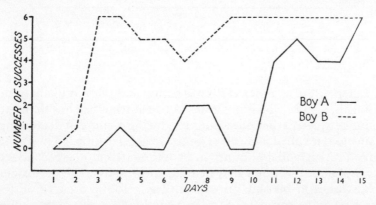

FIG. 1. Learning to do an upstart at the end of the parallel bars. The exercise was demonstrated before each practice session and six trials were made each day. Based on figures given by C. L. Bowdlear, 1927.

7

to the units of measurements used, it is important to be aware of the types which the learner may experience.

First there may be a period during which no measurable learning occurs. This is shown in Fig. 1 as a horizontal line in the case of Boy A. A great deal is probably going on within the organism at this time but there is no overt evidence of it.

Then there may be a period during which the gains between later trials are greater than the gains between earlier ones with the result that a curve of increasing gains (often called a curve of positive acceleration) is produced. The first part of the curve in Fig. 2 shows increasing gains. This type of curve may be expected when the task is difficult for the beginner. It is therefore most likely to be met when young children are trying to learn new skills or in the initial stages of acquiring a skill which is wholly alien to the learner.

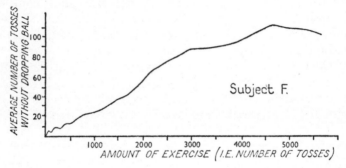

FIG. 2. From E. L. Thorndike, 1913, and after E. J. Swift, 1903.

Later where complex skills are concerned there is likely to be a long period in which the gains between trials are less than the gains between earlier ones, thus producing a curve of decreasing gains (often called a curve of negative acceleration). This is the curve which will be found most frequently at the secondary level of education or when dealing with an average performer who wishes to become an expert. Fig. 3 shows a curve of decreasing gains and part of the curve in Fig. 2 is also of this kind.

Krueger[4] conducted an experiment to show how the difficulty of a task influenced the curves of learning. The task consisted of tossing rings on to a nail in a wall 4 feet from the

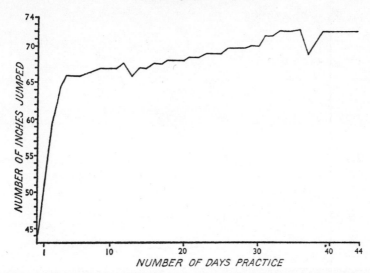

FIG. 3. Standing broad jump of one woman. N. C. Fannin, 1925.

ground from varying distances. As can be seen in Fig. 4, the group of twenty students who pitched from 2 feet learned quickly and soon achieved perfection. The curve was one of decreasing gains. In the case of the group who threw from 3 feet the trend was almost in a straight line with possibly a trace of positive acceleration changing towards negative acceleration at the end. The 6-feet group made increasing gains and the 9-feet group almost no gain. These four curves of learning may show different phases of a general curve. When the requirement is difficult for the learner the pattern is one of increasing gains but as the learner gets nearer to the goal the pattern changes to one of decreasing gains.

Assuming that an individual persists in his efforts, a curve of decreasing gains for any skill will ultimately level off at the goal of perfection or at the physiological limit of the individual. Perfection in the complex skills of physical education and physical recreation is virtually impossible. It is also probably rare in practice for an individual to reach his physiological limit which may be defined as that level of performance beyond which, by reason of the physical limitations of his particular organism, an individual cannot go. It has been found for

9

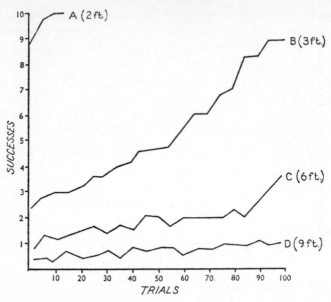

F IG. 4. Pitching rings on to a nail from varying distances as shown. Averages of 20 students in each case. W. C. F. Krueger, 1947.

example that years of practice at such skills as telegraphy or typesetting do not commonly bring a man to his maximal performance. The introduction of a special incentive may improve performance quite remarkably. In 1937 Woodworth[5] wrote that: 'A good example of the physiological limit is seen in the hundred yards' dash since apparently no one can lower the record much below 10 seconds.' The world record now stands at 9.3 seconds, an improvement of 7 per cent. In events where methods not only of training but also of skill performance can be changed, improvement has been even more apparent. The fact that athletic and swimming records are repeatedly being broken is an indication of the practical remoteness of a physiological limit. It may safely be concluded that in normal persons a physiological limit is not reached by ordinary amounts of practice and indeed may not be reached even by intensive and continuous training under favourable conditions.

It will however be argued that many people reach a level of

performance where no improvement is shown with further repetitions. Levels of this kind appearing between the initial level and the physiological limit are known as plateaux or periods of arrested progress. Intermediate levels of this kind occur frequently in the learning of the complex skills with which this book is largely concerned.

A plateau is a period during which, although there are fluctuations from trial to trial, there is no definite change in the performance as measured. The trend towards further gains ceases, even though practice is continued. Although in some cases improvement may really be continuing though not apparent to the learner, a plateau is very discouraging and Kitson[6] has appropriately called it a 'plateau of despond'. If effort continues long enough this period of stagnation is passed sometimes in a sudden burst of ability that carries the learner to a much higher level of attainment. The classical example of this was given by Bryan and Harter[7] who examined the records of students of telegraphy learning to receive messages. For many weeks there was an improvement which the student could feel sure of and which was proved by objective tests. Then followed a long period lasting in many cases for as long as two months during which there was no apparent progress. This was in spite of the fact that the level attained was commercially unacceptable so that the student tried very hard to improve, or to put it another way, he was very highly motivated. If the student persisted in his efforts the plateau ended with a sudden considerable increase in his rate of receiving messages. It is worth noting however that some students became so discouraged by the plateau that they gave up altogether.

A more interesting example, since it involved a game with a ball, is illustrated by Fig. 5. The game consisted essentially 'of throwing a rubber ball into a target on the wall or in causing it to bounce into a target on the floor. These two items could be practised separately or together and with the right hand only or alternatively with the right and left hands'. The period of arrested progress 'was arbitrarily defined to include any period during which the score did not improve for six or more successive practices'.[8]

When learning any complex physical skill such as lawn tennis or swimming it seems to the learner as if progress

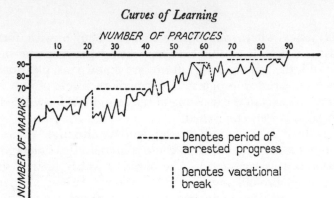

FIG. 5. Ringball, Type 2, Curve of subject M.V. from M. Drury
Smith, 1930.

usually consists of periods of noticeable improvement interspersed by plateaux of varying lengths. Many people seem to
stay permanently on the first or second plateau though this is
rarely their physiological limit. Lack of progress may be due to
discouragement and a lack of incentive or desire, to inadequate
instruction or example, or may arise because the learner believes he has reached his physiological limit.

*Causes of plateaux*

It is advantageous to avoid plateaux where possible because
they are so discouraging. It is advisable therefore to examine
the causes of plateaux more closely. Some psychologists 'regard the plateau as due to factors inherent in the learning process' and others 'suppose it to be the result of a temporary
failure in attention and effort on the part of the subject'.[9]
These views are not of course mutually exclusive. Plateaux do
not usually occur when a relatively simple act is being learned
and even in relatively complex activities they do not necessarily
arise. Nevertheless in skills of physical education and physical
recreation they often do occur.

When a person starts to learn a new skill he frequently begins
with a tremendous amount of enthusiasm and interest. At the
same time he may find that he is able to use his experience in
similar skills to advantage and he probably learns the easier
parts of the skill first. Progress therefore is obvious and seems
very rapid. Gradually the rate of improvement slows down.

The very fact that improvement is slower and not very apparent is discouraging to many people – one meets in England many dabblers who never get past this stage – and the resultant depression may cause a plateau. The slow rate of progress may also make the activity 'not worth the candle' to the person concerned and he will then cease to progress through lack of interest and incentive. On occasions too a plateau arises when a skill is not quite automatic but the learner is over-confident, feels the task is easy and so does not concentrate as hard as he should.

Another important cause of plateaux are the bad habits which may have been acquired during learning and which prevent further progress. A squash racket player may make an unnecessary movement, such as pointing his racket at the ball as it comes off the front wall, which will give him too little time to perform a good stroke. A boxer may always make some habitual movement before using a particular punch thereby telegraphing his intentions to his opponent. A swimmer of the crawl stroke may get into the habit of over-reaching and pulling across the centre-line thereby causing excessive rolling. In order to make a further advance, such habits must be eliminated and the process of elimination frequently involves a considerable lowering of performance for a time. Many people are not willing to face this period of set-back and therefore limit their improvement permanently.

A plateau may also arise when the limit attainable with the method being used has been reached. For example, the 'frying-pan' grip for the service in lawn tennis has a limiting effect at a relatively low level of performance and a person using the 'scissors' technique at high jumping will not jump as great a height with the same amount of spring as he would if he satisfactorily learned the Western Roll.

Since plateaux are in themselves discouraging, every effort should be made to avoid them and this is true even if it results in the initial progress being slower. A teacher or coach can help greatly by encouragement and particularly by technical advice. As bad habits and methods which limit progress at a later date are important causes of plateaux, good form should be taught from the very beginning. By good form is meant a style or technique which is a good basis for future development and which will not limit that particular individual in his acquisition of the skill, in his building up of the ability to produce the desired result with maximum certainty. Good form refers to fundamentals rather than to detail and it must be thought of in terms of the individual concerned. A technique suitable for one may be limiting for another with different physical or mental attributes. This need to avoid bad habits and inadequate methods means that a person wishing to learn a new skill should have expert instruction from the very beginning. Indeed it is probably of more importance at this stage of the learning process than at any other.

But although many plateaux can be avoided by means of good teaching it appears possible that some are inherent in the learning process itself and therefore cannot be evaded. The knowledge that this is so may help the learner through these discouraging periods.

Bryan and Harter[10] believed that the plateau which they found (see page 11) occurred 'at the region of transition from one order to the next in a hierarchy of habits'. Thus the beginner first learned the alphabet of dots and dashes in terms of patterns of clicks. Later he became familiar with word patterns and later still with phrases. The word habit is a 'higher unit' than a letter habit, the phrase habit is higher still and so on. A learner passes through each stage but he may get periods of arrested progress between the stages. The plateau represents a limit for the act as it is being performed and the subsequent rise to a higher level is the result of using a better and different method.

A similar situation may arise in team games. An individual who learns the techniques first outside the game, then has to learn to use them in the game situation and to anticipate so that he can produce them at the appropriate time. Later again he has to learn to look at the over-all general pattern which involves an appreciation of tactics and strategy. One may view these later stages as 'higher units'. Many people may fail to pass from one stage to the next which means they have stayed on a plateau.

Sometimes too a learner finds that he has lost some of his earlier enthusiasm and tries to make up for it by will-power and excessive effort. This may lead to a lapse from the 'higher unit' stage which he has reached to a more elementary and less valuable method of procedure and a consequent breakdown in performance. Some staleness may be of this type.

There is however some controversy as to whether the type of plateau which Bryan and Harter[11] found is really necessary. If the learner could learn the whole skill from the beginning and not attempt to learn it in parts, then could not these plateaux be avoided? The answer depends on whether or not the skill is too difficult for the learner to acquire without passing through the earlier stages. This matter will be considered again under whole and part learning but meanwhile it should be noted that Smith[12] writes: 'The general conclusion can be drawn with some confidence that in a task which the subject regards as being made up of distinct components or phases, there will generally be periods of arrested progress, but in a task which the subject regards as a unit such periods will probably not occur.' It must however be admitted that in practice plateaux do seem to be normal features of the learning process where complex physical activities are concerned and that much disappointment and frustration will be avoided if both teachers and pupils realize this fact.

A general picture has been drawn of the ways in which progress in skill acquisition may be made and it is now necessary to consider the conditions which determine the speed with which a given level of performance is reached.

# III

## FACTORS AFFECTING THE
## ACQUISITION OF SKILL

THE CONDITIONS which determine the speed with which a given level of performance is reached may be divided into: (1) those which vary with the skill and the methods of acquisition and (2) those which vary with the learner. The latter will be considered in Chapter V.

Of course the skill to be learned and the learner are not sharply divided from each other as this classification seems to imply but interact one with another. What is learned is not purely an external something to be absorbed by the learner but depends largely on what the learner perceives and this again depends on the person concerned. Nevertheless it is convenient for purposes of discussion if they can at this stage be considered separately.

Individuals do however vary greatly one from another and also any particular individual varies from time to time so that any general conclusions which can be reached should be applied with care and without dogmatism. Even the most generally accepted laws may not be applicable to a particular case. Frequently, too, general conclusions cannot be drawn with any certainty because of lack of evidence and in these circumstances only the influencing factors can be pointed out. Here again intelligent use of such information on the part of the teacher, coach or learner is important. With these words of warning, the factors which vary with the skill and the methods of acquisition may now be considered.

## (1) GUIDANCE AND INSTRUCTION

The first point which arises is whether it is better to let a beginner learn a complex skill by trying out the activity and practising it with no advice or instruction or whether learning is more satisfactory if guidance and instruction are given.

The learner if left to himself usually continues to practise the first method which happens to bring him some reward in terms of results. It is very rare for this method to be technically sound. The tennis player faces the net and pushes the ball when he serves, the jumper runs straight at the rope or lathe and so on. The argument that people will learn by their mistakes and find the best way may apply to a few individuals but in the main a person without instruction tends to continue with the method he happens to hit on at first and if this becomes 'grooved' it is extremely difficult to change under later expert tuition. It is very difficult to teach a person to develop a good service at tennis if he has played for a couple of years using the 'frying-pan' grip. Indeed it seems more difficult to modify an initial pattern which has been well practised than to lay it down in the first place.

Cox[13] conducted experiments which are of interest here even though the skills concerned were the industrial ones of assembling, wiring and stripping an electric lamp-holder. A group of boys and a group of adults each performed the required operations at top speed until each day's series had been completed. These two groups were found to make no significantly greater progress than did control groups who only took the initial and final tests. Then another group of adults tried to learn the container operation by repeating it as speedily as they could and after 11 practice sessions their results were compared with another group who were instructed in the general principles underlying the best methods of work and who carried out special exercises designed to draw their attention to points to be observed in manipulating the materials as well as taking part in speed tests. The special exercises drew attention to such things as manner of holding the parts, visual and kinaesthetic cues, control of attention and effort and their application to the whole operation under normal working conditions. The latter group made significantly greater gains than the former in spite of the fact that they repeated the actual process far less times. It should perhaps be pointed out that the term 'significant' is used throughout this book in its statistical sense. This means that one would expect to get similar results if one tried the test again on other random samples drawn from the same population.

His results led Cox to follow Myers'[14] example and distinguish between practice and training. He defined practice as the repetition of an operation more or less mechanically at maximum speed and distinguished it from training in which the learner receives instruction from a competent person and is required to use his reason and intelligence.

When teachers talk of practice they usually mean what Cox called training and the term repetition in this connexion is not meant to imply that the successive performances are exact copies of each other. Indeed if they were exact copies of each other then learning, which implies change, would not be taking place. It is apparent however from observation of individuals practising that the distinction is not always clear to them and that many suffer from the mistaken idea that to go through the motions is enough.

Sheer repetition then does not necessarily result in improvement and the learning of these particular operations was more efficient and rapid when the individuals were not left to their own resources but were given special exercises and verbal guidance. These skills were, however, industrial, and it cannot automatically be assumed that the results are applicable to the learning of gross bodily skills.

Davies[15] however carried out an investigation into the effect of tuition upon the process of learning the complex motor skill of archery. She formed two classes with twenty girls in each. The groups were very similar in terms of height, weight, mental ability, previous physical education experience and motivation. One class was given regular and systematic instruction in the technique of archery of the type commonly presented by teachers of this sport. The other group practised under the observation of the experimenter but without instruction other than the minimum amount necessary for the manipulation of the equipment with safety. There were two periods of 50 minutes each for 9 weeks and the results in terms of scores are given in Fig. 6.

It can be seen that (a) the curves both show decreasing gains and are similar in pattern, (b) the class receiving skilled instruction learned faster than did the non-tuition group during both the initial and later stages of learning.

Davies also made the following points which are of interest: (1) The tuition group were given instructions in technique before they shot their first arrows. They started at a higher level of performance.

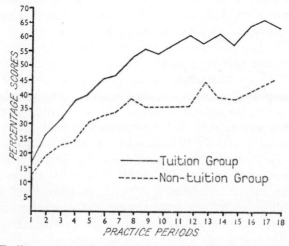

Fɪɢ. 6. Daily average percentage scores for the two archery groups.
D. R. Davies, 1945.

(2) None of the learning curves for individuals were alike. There was marked variation from day to day and even within any practice period. Tuition had no noticeable effect on these irregularities.

(3) Competition seemed to act as an incentive for the instructed subjects whose scores rose on all but the last tournament day, but it was not so effective for the uninstructed group whose imperfectly organized skill tended to break down under the somewhat greater strain of competition.

(4) The tuition group was much more flexible in acquiring form. Thus the non-tuition group acquired a fairly successful

19

technique – successful in terms of scores at that stage – and were then unwilling to try any other form whereas the tuition group were willing to attempt change when suggested by the instructor even though there was a temporary loss in score. This last observation is a particularly important one. Apparently teaching increased the flexibility of behaviour and prevented the learner from falling into a set pattern which brought some immediate success but which produced results far below his potentialities.

These experiments of Cox and Davies suggest that merely playing a game or running around a track are inefficient ways of acquiring skill. But whether training is a better way or not will depend on the quality and form of the instruction.

Welford[16] has pointed out that the way in which a task 'is performed the first time it is met may largely determine the manner of its performance subsequently'. Since this means that the first performance of a new skill is likely to be of crucial importance to its later development, great care must be taken in the learning situation to set the stage so that the learner will get as near as he can to the best solution at his first attempt. Once an individual knows what specific skill he wishes to learn the so-called 'natural' way is not the best. It is true that a person can learn from his mistakes but it is better to learn from the mistakes of others who have gone before and to start as far on as possible towards the perfect skill. Begin in the right way is sound advice; it is not a good idea in acquiring a specific skill to let the beginner 'have a bash' and struggle along making unnecessary mistakes. Good instruction saves the learner's time for it helps to prevent the formation of bad habits or the use of technically unsound methods which would hold him back later on and which would probably be overcome only with the greatest difficulty. 'To break up a bad method is more than double the task of teaching a wholly untrained child'.[17] Often a bad habit acquired in the early days of learning a skill and subsequently eradicated will reappear when an athlete is under the extreme pressure of competition at a high level.

Even with good advice the learner must 'have a go' and he must proceed by trial and error. He is bound to make many mistakes and his movements will often be clumsy and in poor form. Such movements must not be allowed to become habitual and the learner should be encouraged to vary his actions until he happens to hit upon some pattern of movements in accordance with good form. When a person is learning a skill he frequently tends to try to correct his mistakes by going too far in the opposite direction. This method of reaching the ideal is probably a good one but in some activities the learner has to be encouraged to make this variation. A person who is afraid of making mistakes is unlikely to get very far. For instance in racket games some of the best services are those which land or would land on or close to the lines of the service court. But because the server is penalized heavily if he puts the ball or shuttle out he frequently plays safe and does not vary his attempts sufficiently to hit upon the best technique. Similarly a person who wishes to become an expert at racing dinghies may have to capsize once or twice in order to learn the extremes to which he can safely go.

Having made the mistakes, however, the learner should be worried by them and it is in discarding incorrect solutions that progress will be made. The teacher can help by discouraging wrong movements before they become habitual, by suggesting new behaviour, by encouraging experimentation and variation in the early stages and by leaving the right movements undisturbed when they appear. But the teacher, when he suggests new behaviour, cannot lay down the law about this because a suggestion which proves the key to one individual may not help another individual at all. A good performer often thinks that the keys which have helped him to translate words into actions will automatically prove of value to others. Sometimes they may do so but there is no guarantee of this. More often some other idea or suggestion or gesticulation is necessary to get the learner to acquire good form. The more meaningful the skill is to him, the easier it is for him to learn it and the less errors he is likely to make.

In the investigations by Cox[18] and Davies[19] various kinds of instruction were utilized and so it is now necessary to inquire into the relative efficacy of different means used to make the skill more meaningful. These include visual and manual guidance, and verbal directions both oral and written.

## A. VISUAL GUIDANCE

The fundamental form of visual guidance is demonstration which is valuable at all levels of skill provided the demonstration is a good one. The beginner needs a clear idea of the whole skill which he is trying to achieve and this can be obtained most satisfactorily from seeing an expert in action. He will then have a general idea of the patterns involved and the circumstances in which the movements are appropriate. If this is not possible then the teacher or coach can give a demonstration. But there are dangers inherent in demonstration. When a person demonstrates he tends to show what he thinks is done instead of what actually is done in the real situation. It was Gilbreth,[20] of motion study fame, who first discovered this. He found that bricklayers when doing identically the same type of work had three different sets of motions. Set 1 was used to teach the beginner, set 2 was used when working slowly and set 3 when working rapidly. At one time many tennis coaches used to demonstrate the playing of a low ball at tennis with a method never in fact used by top-class players in match play.

The importance of the demonstration being a good one raises the question of the standard of performance of the teacher. Ragsdale[21] has said that 'since the learner sees only the general form of the activity, undue concern about perfection of the model seems out of place'. This author does not agree. The early stages in skill learning are vital to future progress and the essence of most complex skills of the type found in physical education and physical recreation is timing. The impression of this can be given by a competent performer. A demonstrator who can play the game or perform the act competently can continually refer back to what is done in actual performance. A person on the other hand who cannot perform adequately himself may be teaching the skill demonstrated – which may be different from the skill wanted – or even be merely teaching the skill of demonstrating.

But if the teacher feels his own performance is of too low a standard he can give a clear idea of the whole skill to the beginner by showing him a film of the expert performing in competition. Films taken of experts demonstrating are again of doubtful use.

To the beginner the film should be shown at natural speed and not in slow motion so that he can get the 'feel' of the action. Kinaesthesis or 'muscle sense' is very important in learning a skill and many people have the ability to watch a person perform and then do a somewhat similar action without necessarily bringing any conscious effort into it. Such individuals may feel when watching an expert as if they are doing the act and often if they immediately try they can in fact perform it better than they usually can. Anyone who has met spectators returning home in their cars after watching motor-racing will be aware of this. The number who act as if they are Stirling Moss on the track is quite frightening! Again at boxing there are occasions on which members of the audience show fighting ability quite above the ordinary! Seriously though, imitative powers can be used to advantage in skill acquisition. They are particularly strong in children and it is doubtful if enough use is made of them in teaching skills. It is true that the child may copy parts of the techniques which are not necessary – many children copied Pirie's habit of blowing out his cheeks – but they would still make faster, beneficial progress too. If television does not discourage people from 'having a go' then it may prove advantageous for it enables the many to copy the few who have outstanding skill.

The time spent on showing beginners an expert performance should be brief and no analysis should be attempted. They should immediately attempt to perform the skill with occasional looks again at the 'model'. The sole purpose of the demonstration at this stage should be to give the beginner a good idea of the skill he is going to try to attain – and this idea will often be in terms of muscular imagery or kinaesthesis as well as by means of visual imagery.

The contribution of kinaesthesis in skill learning has been brought to particular notice by the results of an experiment conducted by Griffith as reported by Kretchmar *et al.*[22] Blindfolded individuals were taught to drive a golf ball and in the initial weeks their progress was comparable to a control group not using blindfolds. After a period of several weeks the experimental group were permitted to continue their practice without blindfolds and it was then found that their progress was noticeably superior to that of the control group. The enforced use of kinaesthesis in the early stages proved beneficial to later learning in this case. The results from this experiment may not however be generalized. Phillips and Summers[23] state that 'methods of teaching in which awareness of the kinaesthetic sense is emphasized do not appear to be more effective in improving learning than do the more conventional approaches. Coady found that golf skills were not significantly improved by these techniques and McGrath found the same to be true in teaching free-throw shooting'. The interpretation of experimental evidence is complicated by the fact that kinaesthesis appears to consist of many separate and specific capacities.

After the initial stage of learning has been passed, visual aids can be used in a second way to help make the skill more meaningful to the learner. Instead of giving only a general idea of the skill for purposes of imitation – though demonstration for this purpose should still be used from time to time – more attention can be given to detail so that the learner's understanding of the skill may be increased. This can be done in several ways. In the first place, a coach may try to convey the pattern or speed or direction of a movement to a learner by actions rather than words. These actions are not necessarily expert examples of the skill the learner is trying to acquire but are the means by which some feature of technique which the learner has not previously understood may be communicated to him. Such actions might perhaps be termed gesticulations rather than demonstrations.

Secondly analysis can be used. Anderson,[24] for example, found it advantageous to use visual aids in the form of spots on the backboard to teach beginners to shoot at basket-ball. When the learner is really keen on a skill then film analysis of it can help him to gain a deeper understanding. Examination of the films of experts taking part in competition and critical analyses of films of himself or of other less outstanding performers, can be beneficial, particularly to the formulation of principles which can guide him. Principles of this kind are particularly helpful in rebuilding some skill which has been previously learned and which has temporarily broken down.

Analysis is also of great help to those who intend to teach the activity, for it helps to draw attention to fundamental requirements. The teacher is different from the learner for he must be able to recognize skill in others by the way it looks and be able to pick out faults from observation.

Film is particularly useful for analysis purposes because it can be slowed down or stopped without destroying the basic patterns of movement. As has already been pointed out 'live models cannot be used effectively, since slowing down any movement changes the activity pattern and falsifies it as a whole'.[25] Analyses should not only be of the actual movements involved in performing the skill but also of the cues which indicate the need for that particular response and of the tactical settings in which the response is the appropriate one.

Experimental evidence on the value of films is inconclusive.

Priebe and Burton[26] worked with twenty-six adolescent boys and came to the conclusion that the use of films in teaching high jumps resulted in greater improvement and shortened the initial period of trial-and-error learning. Lockhart[27] found that a group learning bowling in a skittle alley with the aid of film avoided plateaux and were still slightly advanced on the control group after seven weeks of instruction. Brown and Messersmith[28] who used film of agilities performed by experienced gymnasts and also by members of the class itself, found indications that the experimental class made a little more progress than the control but the superiority was not statistically significant. They also commented that the filming of the students in the class made them highly motivated. Nelson[29] who studied the effect of slow-motion loopfilms on the learning of the golf swing using a number seven iron, found no significant differences between the control group and the group which had the use of the films. All of these studies were on small numbers and did not take the skill far enough. It is apparent that further research, in which the actual way in which the film is used is more precisely delineated, is required in this area.

### B. MANUAL OR MECHANICAL GUIDANCE

This procedure involves actively pushing the learner's body through the desired movements or providing artificial support so that the technique can be carried out. In general it is not desirable because the kinaesthetic sensations felt by the learner will be different from those he experiences when performing on his own and there is also the risk that he will adopt a passive attitude which is never conducive to learning. Nevertheless there are occasions on which the method is worth trying. Examples are when a learner seems quite incapable of either copying a movement demonstrated to him or translating verbal explanation into movement or when he cannot complete the whole pattern of an action because of some relatively minor difficulty.

It is also of use when the skill is a dangerous one. For example when learning to somersault in the air a harness can be used so that certain aspects of the whole skill can be appreciated in their context without risk. Artificial supports have been found of value in learning to swim provided that they are not used for too long, and provided the techniques are still taught. Kinnear[30] points out that 'with the old class techniques of confidence practices, skill practices at the rail with little or no movement and no artificial aids, the poor children quickly lost any sense of exhilaration, any enjoyment in the activity and naturally lost interest'. With the artificial aid of rings, wings, floats and so on, they can experience the thrill of moving freely in the water in the first lesson. Mechanical or manual guidance if used at all should however be minimal.

## C. VERBAL DIRECTIONS

It must not be assumed automatically that these are beneficial. Since the beginner must have as clear an idea as possible of the skill he is to learn before he starts, a brief verbal description may be of value but the results of an experiment by Battig[31] suggest that the value of verbal pre-training decreases as the complexity of the actual motor responses increases. When the motor side of a skill is relatively unimportant and it is a case rather of noticing changes in the environment and reacting correctly to them, then verbal pre-training can be valuable. An example of this might be in sailing where the actual movements are relatively simple and the skill is rather in the ability to interpret the needs of the situation. When the motor aspect is very complex, then preliminary verbal training is apparently of little use. It seems likely therefore that in most of the activities of physical education, talking about the actual movements before they have been experienced will not be very helpful.

Again it cannot be automatically assumed that verbal training will be beneficial after the movements have been experienced.

Thus it has been clearly shown in the learning of the manipulatory skill of keeping a stylus in contact with a moving 'bead' that verbal instruction given at the beginning of each practice period was detrimental to the acquisition of the skill.[32] This, of course, refers to pursuit learning and does not therefore necessarily apply to skills involving big muscle groups.

Goodenough and Brian[33] conducted an interesting experiment in which twenty four-and-a-half year-old-children, divided into three sub-groups, were trained for fifty days in throwing rings over a post set at a distance of 4 feet $10\frac{1}{2}$ inches. The ten children in Group A were given no instruction or criticism with regard to their methods of throwing; the six in Group B were given a brief preliminary demonstration and a subsequent verbal criticism of the general types of errors made; the four in Group C were given the same treatment as Group B *but* they were also taught to follow a definite procedure in throwing and were not allowed to experiment. Results showed that the amount of improvement averaged least for Group A, only slightly higher for Group B but very much greater for Group C. These results indicate that the best procedure is to enforce from the start a given effective method (this provides further evidence to support what was said on page 20) and to combine this with verbal guidance after the first attempt. This and other experiments concerned with gross bodily skills were conducted on a very small scale and other conditions besides verbal directions were varied so that it is not possible to draw general conclusions or evaluate the contribution of verbal instruction *per se*.

Verbal directions must not be overdone particularly when dealing with young children or beginners because of the difficulties of comprehension. Goodenough and Brian pointed out that to one of the children in their experiment 'being careful' meant 'being very gentle or cautious' and to another 'trying hard' was synonymous with 'throwing with great violence'. If a teacher tries to describe movements reasonably accurately he tends to take rather a long time and use technical terms unfamiliar to the learner. This may create feelings of uncertainty, frustration or boredom and so impede learning. Attempts have been made to draw up a language of movement but one universally accepted has not yet been produced. The problem of conveying movements in words is particularly difficult because the individual is not normally conscious of his actions when his skill is working well. Linguistic problems are too complex for discussion in this book.

27

In the early stages then verbal directions should be brief and should be used mainly to direct observation. Detailed descriptions of movements should be avoided and it should always be remembered that the pupil learns only if he actively perceives, thinks and plans during the instruction.

As the learner progresses or gets older and more generally experienced, verbal directions and analysis of movement can help more in increasing the meaningfulness of the skill and in giving new insights into it. Reasons for particular movements, provided that the reasons are within the comprehension of the learner, help a person to correct his own actions not only at the time but subsequently. It might perhaps be advisable to consider here the extent to which knowledge of principles may be expected to influence the learning of motor skills.

It has been seen that an explanation of general principles was included in the 'training' sessions by Cox[34] but as special exercises were also carried out the value of the former is not clear. Judd[35] gave one group of boys, aged approximately eleven and twelve years, instruction in the principle of refraction. He then compared their ability to hit with darts a target placed 12 inches under water with a comparable group who had received no instruction. The groups were equally successful. Theory therefore seemed of no value in the first instance for all boys had to learn how to use the dart and theory proved no substitute for practice. When however the target was put at 4 inches under the water the difference between the groups was striking. Those who had had no theory were very confused and made large and persistent errors whereas the other group dealt with the new depth very rapidly. Theory therefore was of no value until backed by practical experience but when theory and practice were both present new adjustments were rapidly made. This early work by Judd was by modern standards inadequately reported.

Hendrickson and Schroeder[36] carried out a rather similar experiment using an air-gun instead of darts. Although they confirmed that knowledge of theory facilitated transfer, some of their other results were at variance with those of Judd.[37] They found indications that the theoretical information did help the initial adjustment to the problem – though the results were not statistically reliable – and they also found that improvement occurred both with and without tuition. In this experiment the motor response or technique was a negligible factor in the skill for once a boy had discovered where to aim he had no difficulty in hitting the target. It seems highly probable that in Judd's experiment the subjects had to learn to throw darts as well as adapt to refraction and this would help to explain the difference in the results.

Colville[38] criticized these two experiments because instruction was included in such a way that the group receiving it was allotted additional time. She therefore selected three principles of mechanics and three motor skills each of which utilized one of the principles One group of female students practised the skill and was taught to understand and apply the principles and a comparable group spent the same amount of time learning the skills without reference to the principle involved. The performances of the groups were compared in each skill and also in another skill in which the same general principles applied. The skills were ballrolling, catching a tennis ball in a lacrosse stick and a badminton bird on a tennis racket, and archery. A significant amount of learning took place under both methods and was not only similar in amount but also in pattern. This experiment therefore produced no evidence to support the contention that instruction concerning mechanical principles utilized in the performance of a motor skill facilitates either initial learning of a skill, or subsequent learning as evidenced in the performance of a similar or more complicated skill to which the same principle is applicable, more than an equivalent amount of time spent in practising the skill. The experiment also showed that some part of the learning period could be spent on instruction in principles without detriment to motor learning.

The conclusion which may be drawn from these experiments is that knowledge of principles does not help an individual to learn a particular movement or act but it may help him to transfer that act to other situations at the appropriate moment. To put it another way, if the principles refer to the technique, to the actual movements which the individual is trying to make, then knowledge of them is not beneficial but if the principles refer, as in the second part of Judd's[39] experiment, to the circumstances in which a particular movement is to be made then knowledge of them may help.

It also seems likely that when a skill has been learned a knowledge of principles may aid retention. Performance of complex skills which have been learned, varies from day to day. An individual who knows the underlying principles of his skill can, when his skill is not as good as usual, refer to these principles in his mind and may possibly find the key to his falloff in performance. The principles form a frame of reference which is a useful aid to re-formation of the skill. Similarly in the quite different case of teaching a skill, an understanding of mechanics and a knowledge of underlying principles may help the coach to distinguish between personal idiosyncrasies which do not matter and important fundamentals.

It may be concluded then that guidance and instruction is generally beneficial provided it is well-informed and appropriate to the state of the learner. Ultimately, however, the learner must perform without the help of the coach and therefore, after the first few times, the instruction should be interspersed with longer and longer periods of practice without technical help. Every teacher or coach must beware of the learner becoming too dependent on him although it is always useful for an individual, however expert, to have someone to whom to refer when problems arise. But the initiative should rest with the performer.

Thus Whilden[40] taught two groups of thirty-seven and thirty-eight girls the rules, fundamental skills and basic tactics of basketball. After six periods of this one group was put completely on its own and the teacher served as consultant only, whereas the other group was completely under the control of the teacher. Four observers rated the players during the fifteenth class period and, after the sixteenth, games were held. The teacher-dominated group received a higher rating on basic skills. The pupil-dominated group showed greater knowledge of the rules, performed better as a team and won three games out of four played against the teacher-dominated group.

Unfortunately most of the research into learning methods deals with the early stages only and thus the effects of instruction in the long run are not clear experimentally. The views of the author are the following.

Where the contribution of the technique or motor aspect of skill to the end result is very great then instruction plays a large part in improvement even when the performer's standard is high. These skills include such activities as olympic gymnastics, diving, the throwing and jumping events in athletics, and swimming.

When one comes to the activities where reaction to the external environment is extremely important, self-instruction and discovery become more valuable. Good instruction in the early stages into the fundamentals of the personal skills involved is beneficial and in the case of the ordinary person vital, but this need not be carried on for so long. In team and racket games the ability to see which particular personal skill is required in rapidly changing situations is what makes a skilled player. Although instruction can help here, any individual who makes an intelligent approach to the game can probably learn as quickly on his own. A teacher can however be very useful in creating situations which present the learner with tactical problems and in helping him to solve those problems in terms of the learner's abilities and attitude to the game.

There seems to be a fundamental difference of approach between, say, learning to shot-putt and learning to play tennis. In the former, physical attributes determine results to a large extent whereas in games like tennis, football, and cricket, physical attributes are not so obvious and are certainly more varied. One has only to think of Nieder, O'Brien, Rowe, Lindsay on the one hand and Kramer, Falkenburg, Savitt, Hoad, Rosewall on the other. Having an individual with the necessary physical attributes on which to build, the teacher of shot-putting can teach him good form from the first and any new variations of technique are likely to be discovered by the expert rather than the novice. Talking of the athletic genius, Bartlett[41] says 'the genius in skilled movement, like the genius in other fields, is the man who is continually experimenting with what he has been taught'. The coach can have in his mind a model of the expert shot-putter and build up his athlete accordingly. In team and racket games this is a dangerous attitude. If one examines the top performers in professional lawn tennis there are great differences in their play – technically, tactically and temperamentally. Hoad with his wristy shots, spins and power, Segura with his two-handed forehand, his subtlety and tactical sense, Rosewall with his all-round soundness and running ability all demonstrate the wide differences which are possible in the great player. The motor aspects alone, though showing similar basic fundamentals also show great variations. Similarly if an English international association football team is examined a great diversity of physiques and styles will usually be found. Probably there will be some individuals who are strong, thrustful and direct in their play;

others will depend more on agility and subtlety. Some players will rely on speed and others on good positioning. Indeed the art of building a team lies in the ability to blend the various styles and temperaments of the players so that the outstanding skills of each may be utilized to the full and so as to produce a unique force greater than the individuals from which it is composed (see Plates 3, 4, 5 and 6).

Here then instruction must take the form of building on the interests, abilities and temperament of each individual rather than having a model in one's mind and selecting or encouraging those persons who can attain to that model. The teacher after the initial stages – a good groundwork in basic fundamentals is still important – must help the individual to develop his individuality. It is possible that in many cases an individual can develop his individuality equally well on his own. Certainly instruction must be good to be beneficial and it is suggested that good instruction for the games player and for other activities where adjustment to rapidly changing situations must be made should be different from good instruction in the case of personal skills which do not have to adjust to any great extent to external requirements.

The function of instruction is always to prepare the situation and chain of events so that there is a maximum possibility of the learner acquiring the desired skill. 'Learning is done by the learner and not by some kind of transmission process from the teacher.'[42]

## (2) KNOWLEDGE OF RESULTS

If a person practises without knowing the results of his actions, improvement in his performance is unlikely. Lindsley[43] reported 'that a group of radar operators who were not enlightened about their progress on successive trials became less and less accurate as practice went on for six days'. Knowledge of results serves as a guide to the learner in his subsequent practices and functions as a basis of selection of what is good in that performance. The knowledge should be as exact as possible. In a study by Trowbridge and Cason[44] involving line-drawing it was shown that blindfolded subjects who, as soon as possible after each trial, were told the amount and direction of error improved much more than did those who were told simply whether the line was right or wrong. Other experiments in practical skills agree that the learner should be given as specific and as immediate information as possible.

Many skills in physical education and physical recreation provide in themselves some knowledge of results. The tennis ball is hit or missed, the discus is thrown 170 or 90 feet, the goal is scored or it is not. But during the learning process in each and every case one must ask if the information is given as soon as it can be and if it is as specific as possible. This problem was put in a nutshell by Guthrie[45] when he said that if only a golfer could receive a sharp pain at the point when he goes wrong in his swing and slices the ball he would stop doing it. But seeing the effects of the slice some moments after the swing is finished makes adjustment a much more difficult problem. A coach with good observational powers who is dealing with one or two individuals only can help to give information at critical moments. It is a far more difficult problem for the teacher of a large class. More precise information can sometimes be obtained by the individual learners if they carry out exercises planned for this purpose. For example a large number of people in a class may be unable to smash in a game of tennis even though they appear to smash well enough when practising. Various exercises can be set up which will reveal where the weaknesses lie. The ball may be lobbed from different parts of the court to a relatively stationary receiver or the ball may be lobbed so that the receiver has to move backwards or forwards or backwards and sideways. It may then be found that the individual can deal with the smashes except when he has to run backwards. This may mean that he must get confidence in his ability to run backwards before he can smash in the game – particularly as these are the circumstances in which the smash is usually met.

In team games it is always difficult to give adequate knowledge of results to each individual. The person in team games who goes on improving is often the one who can best assess the results of his own actions. Thus when a man passes a ball to someone on his own side and that individual fails to get it he must be able to decide if it was his fault or that of the person to whom he has passed. Part of a teacher's job in team games is to help players analyse the results of their actions. In school netball one finds frequently that the thrower of the ball and the person who has failed to get it are each blaming the other and so no progress results. When an individual begins to acknowledge his own failures he can start making efforts to correct those failures. Sometimes a centre court player at netball will fail continually to pass the ball to one girl even though she is free. By isolating the situation and practising it on its own it may be discovered that the centre court player cannot do the type of pass needed and therefore she must go right back to technique. At other times it may be found to be due to a lack of perception, to an inability to judge that the girl is free. In this case the isolation of the situation will probably have called attention to the cues sufficiently for the centre player to realize in future that the girl is free when the particular set-up arises.

Tests against the stop-watch or tape-measure are often made when teaching athletics. Tests can also be used to aid knowledge of results in other physical activities. A hockey player's power of hitting can be seen by measuring the distance of his hit; his control of the ball and his shooting accuracy by using tests like those outlined by Scott and French.[46] A person who wishes to learn on his own can do a great deal by intelligent self-testing and may indeed make fast progress through developing a highly sensitive appreciation of his own weaknesses and strengths. He must learn to check the result against his intentions. Thus a tennis player should not get satisfaction merely because he wins the point. If he serves an ace but the ball has gone nowhere near where he intended it to go then his skill is not good but bad and he should get no pleasure from it. Similarly in the case of a goal scored by a mis-kick or mis-hit no matter how much public acclaim the scorer may receive.

Sometimes however, and particularly in the beginning, one may want a pupil to learn good form and for the time being ignore the end product. For instance in order to learn the throwing action in the tennis service it may be better in the early stages not to perform on the court otherwise one gets the individual playing safe and pushing or patting the ball so that it will go into the service court.

When paying attention to form it is necessary for the learner to have knowledge of performance, of how he is performing the task, rather than knowledge of results. It is clear that there must be some internal knowledge of results which enables an individual to recognize his more successful attempts and relate them to the way in which they have been achieved. Crossman, Seymour *et al*[47] have suggested that the subject's criterion of achievement and selection may be based not only on outward results but also on energy expenditure. A good attempt may be recognized therefore because it involves less activity and a better performance may be attained 'by the pursuit of increasing laziness'. If the learner has good performers to compare himself with he may be able to improve through self-observation. But more usually he needs the aid of a teacher who can help him at this stage by praise when his form shows improvement and by making him realize that he has indeed made a skilled movement. It is surprising how often a beginner does not realize that he has.

It has previously been pointed out that when the learner happens to hit upon the right movement the teacher must recognize it as such and leave it undisturbed. This implies that the teacher has a considerable depth of knowledge of the particular skill, for the right movement will not be identical for each individual. The movement must be mechanically sound but it will vary from person to person because of differing physiques and underlying qualities. One cannot expect a short person to do a tennis service in the same way as a tall one. And if an individual is relatively stiff in the shoulders and supple in the hips the teacher of the flik-flak will utilize the movement at the hips to the full. If on the other hand the learner is stiff in the hips and supple in the shoulders the movements to be accentuated will be different. A teacher must not try to impose a too precise and specific technique. He must continually be differentiating between the fundamental requirements of technique and the idiosyncrasies of personal style. The latter should be left alone unless they are obviously unsound.

In general, knowledge of bad points helps a person to break down old habits, and knowledge of good points to build up the new. When building up therefore, criticism should be used sparingly and the good points more often praised. But when there is a wish to change a person's technique because it is limiting his progress, criticism is of value for it helps to create in the learner dissatisfaction with his current movements. A movement which has been done for some time feels right to the learner and this feeling must be eradicated. Sometimes telling a person that something is wrong does not convince him. A person with poor posture may have to be convinced of the need for improvement by the aid of mirrors or posture-recorder. A story used to be told of a swimmer who always swam with a certain part of his anatomy out of the water. Telling him had no effect and a catapult had to be used to convince him!

Suppose then that a high-jumper wishes to change from scissors to Western Roll. He must for a time be concerned not with the height he jumps but with his method. But the old technique will tend to feel pleasurable and the new technique awkward. This makes the teacher all-important for he can help break down the old by his criticism and build up the new by his information concerning the performance. For a time knowledge of performance, that is the amount of success with the new style, must come from the teacher. This knowledge should be given at the moment something good is done or a mistake in the movement is made and not afterwards. A cry of appreciation or a yell of horror at the appropriate moment may work wonders! The closer the exclamation is to the good movement or the error the easier it is for the learner to identify the right and wrong actions.

A teacher should not only have a deep knowledge of the skill which he is trying to impart but he should also realize the deficiencies in his own powers of observation. The mind is a faulty instrument. Bartlett [48] has pointed out that 'the number of items that most people can visually observe in a single glance is 5 to 7' and that 'the upper parts and the left-hand portions of a visual field are on the whole the easiest to observe, and anything contained in them on the whole most accurately reported'. The mind is not reliable if it is required to estimate or measure single magnitudes of any kind. Large errors will usually be made in estimating the height, weight, length, position or speed of movement of any object.

The mind is able to make comparative judgements much more easily but even here it has its limitations. This is quite easy to demonstrate. If two people watch ten others run a potato race one after the other and then try to place them in rank order of time taken it will normally be found that the two do not agree with each other and that neither agree with the rank order based on actual stop-watch reading. Usually the disagreements will be substantial. A test of this type in which the testees have shuttled forward and back between skittles three times to complete a hundred yards' run has been carried out annually for many years by the author's students and no one has ever yet produced the correct rank order from observation. Yet how often do we rely on similar types of observation in Physical Education?

The mind finds it difficult to discriminate between small differences, such as the curves of the back in postural assessments, and it can also be misled. Illusions of one kind or another are quite common. How often do we judge that a ball has been struck very hard because the striker obviously makes a great effort? Yet the ball may in fact travel faster and farther when it is struck with the sweetness of good timing and relatively little effort is apparently involved.

Heinlein[49] points out that it is extremely difficult to observe the exact rhythmic nature of the responses of young children to musical patterns during walking, marching, skipping and dancing exercises. In experiments it was found that observations on the rhythmic capacities of several children were quite wrong. Thus one child who was expected to produce a poor performance revealed a strong rhythmic sense and it is suggested that the observer had been biased in his judgement by the child's unhelpful emotional attitudes. Another child who was expected to be the best of the group proved to be very poor. Heinlein states that 'an observer may be easily illusioned to judge an unusual energetic display of motor activity following musical stimulation as a rhythmic response, when in reality no simple mathematical relation may ever exist between the bodily movements and the musical tempo'.

In these experiments it was also found that most observers found it impossible to tap on a key in time with a child's steps which were not necessarily in time with the music. Instead the observer found himself tending to tap in time with the beat of the music.

It was also discovered that there was often an illusion that the children were keeping in exact time with the music when in fact the musician was actually keeping in time with the movements of the children.

Difficulties of observation are experienced by experts as well as by laymen. Jones[50] reports experiments into the reliability of the clinical assessments of nutrition by doctors.

The results in Table 1 are typical.

TABLE 1.

| Nutrition | Doctor 1 | | Doctor 2 | | Doctor 3 | | Doctor 4 | | Doctor 5 | |
|---|---|---|---|---|---|---|---|---|---|---|
| | *1st* | *2nd* | *1st* | *2nd* | *1st* | *2nd* | *1st* | *2nd* | *1st* | *2nd* |
| A (Excellent) | 36 | 48 | 16 | 23 | 8 | 14 | 20 | 32 | 12 | 18 |
| B (Normal) | 146 | 142 | 137 | 147 | 133 | 147 | 83 | 71 | 124 | 129 |
| C (Subnormal) | 11 | 3 | 40 | 23 | 52 | 32 | 76 | 77 | 57 | 45 |
| D (Bad) | — | — | — | — | — | — | 14 | 13 | — | 1 |

These results were obtained from examinations of 193 children in two schools one of which had generally good nutrition and the other poor. The same children were examined by the same five doctors on two occasions with one week between them. On the first occasion the good school was visited first and on the second the children at the poor school were the first to be examined.

The results show clearly that substantial differences occurred between individual doctors and also, except perhaps in the case of Doctor 4, between the observations of any one doctor on the same child on different occasions. Jones stated that in more than half the cases the doctors failed to agree over the crucial question of whether a boy was satisfactorily nourished or not.

It may also be noticed that on the second occasion every doctor found more boys excellently nourished and with the exception of Doctor 4 fewer subnormally nourished. This looks then as if the standards of the doctors were influenced by the change of order in the schools visited and draws attention to the impossibility of keeping fixed standards in the mind. Another example of this has been given by Krumboltz and Christal[51] who analysed results of aviation cadets over a six-year period. They found that a cadet had a better chance of success if he was grouped with cadets of relatively lower aptitude than himself rather than with cadets of relatively higher aptitude. The same kind of problem arises when making team selections. An individual playing in a poor team may appear much better than he does when he is with a better group. In other words the setting has an affect on what is observed. The eyes see but the person perceives for he interprets the sensory information which he receives. This interpretation is influenced by his previous experience and by his personal attitudes and interests. Witnesses of the same accident may give quite different versions even when they are telling the truth. Man is very suggestible. It was the appreciation of this fact which led to Hitlerian propaganda and which is put to good use every day in advertising. The clapping and booing of an audience can easily affect a person's judgements one way or the other.

Man is also often prejudiced and if he approaches a situation with a preconceived idea he may well only see those points which confirm his view. When a hockey or football team is being selected it is easy to think 'bad luck' when a person who you believe to be good does something bad and to continue to watch for him to take action which is up to the standard you expect of him. On the other hand when someone you do not think much of does something bad then it is tempting to think that that proves he is a poor player and ignore anything good which he does from then on.

In order then to make his observations as useful and accurate as is humanly possible a teacher should take every opportunity to check them and particularly against objective measures or tests. He should be constantly aware of the limitations of his observations and be continually alert against suggestion and prejudice.

In many complex skills action is too fast for the detail to be observed by the human eye and other aids to analysis are necessary. Howell[52] has shown for example that a group of ten students who saw force-time graphs of their sprint start immediately after each practice trial showed a highly significant improvement in momentum and speed at the instant they cleared the starting blocks. Another group of ten who were instructed by conventional procedures improved very little. It is probable that with a greater amount of experimentation much could be done to make knowledge of movements more specific.

But even with aids to help observation and the measurement

of results there are some activities where the end-product is not evaluated solely in terms of distance or time or objective score. Thus in olympic gymnastics, diving and dance, qualitative assessments are made. In some forms of dance the skill is employed for aesthetic ends alone. Dance is an art form and the aesthetic ends which it serves do not admit of quantitative determination. Much of the satisfaction is gained purely in performing but where an individual wishes to perfect his skill then the subjective judgements of experienced persons must be available to inform him of the effects of his creations on the onlooker. Only so can he have knowledge of results and thus hope to improve.

In this section knowledge of results and knowledge of performance have been looked at in connexion with learning and therefore in their effect on subsequent acts. The knowledge enables the learner to amend a similar action in a future trial. Only if the knowledge leads to rehearsal with change in posture, movement or action is improvement likely to result. Sometimes over-correction may be made. Most people who have learned to canoe have experienced this in the early stages. The knowledge that they are falling over towards the water on one side causes them to adjust by going too far over to the other. But as has been pointed out before, over-correction is not a bad thing but is merely one step on the way to achieving skill.

Knowledge of the results of the present action can then cause amendment of a later response. Miller,[53] however, has distinguished this use of results from that in which the knowledge enables the learner to amend his present response or adjust subsequent responses in a connected series of actions. This type of effect may make for better performance on that one occasion but may prove detrimental in building up a skill. The long jumper who sees that his run is going to take him over the board can take a short step and thereby complete a jump which counts competitively. This may be better than doing a no-jump on the particular occasion. But if he is practising and trying to improve his skill then such adjustment will not help him for it will gradually build up an unsatisfactory pattern of movement. Similarly a person may make a last second wrist adjustment when serving in tennis and if it is effective in the sense of getting the ball in the court it may become a habit.

This may mean that he will never correct the more fundamental and earlier errors in the stroke. Thus in learning a skill the individual should try to use his knowledge of results and performance after termination of the act in improvement of subsequent similar though not identical movements. In other words it should lead to rehearsal with fundamental improvement. On the other hand when competitively performing it may occasionally pay to use the knowledge in modifying the response as it is made.

## (3) MOTIVATION

Stroud[54] has pointed out that the old maxim that practice makes perfect is a mixture of truth and error because some forms of practice do lead towards perfection but others do not bring about improvement. Practice provides the opportunity for conditions favourable to learning to operate but does not in itself ensure that those conditions shall be present. It has already been observed that sheer repetition does not guarantee improvement and this is understandable for in the initial stages far more wrong movements are repeated than right ones. The 'feeling-tone' which accompanies the act is important. Pleasure when the right movements are made and annoyance at wrong movements aids the acquisition of skills. Knowledge of results helps the individual to identify right and wrong movements and is therefore an integral part of the learning process. But pleasure and annoyance are determined by the individual learner's motivation.

Even with practice under beneficial conditions and with knowledge of results, little improvement will be made if the learner is not interested and does not care about his results. It is the quality of the practice which is important. Unmotivated practice is quite ineffective because complex skills are only learned through intense effort and attention on the part of the learner. Indeed it may be said that the most important factor in skill acquisition is that of motivation.

Motivation will be discussed in more detail in Chapter VI. For the moment only the effect of learning methods on motivation will be considered. Those learning methods which result in steady progress and the avoidance of plateaux are desirable and this means that it is important that bad habits should not be formed and that the first attempts at the skill are on the right lines technically. But the first attempts are also vital in another way. The initial introduction to any activity may colour an individual's attitude to it for a long time if not for ever. This is an obvious truism in the case of swimming where an unfortunate experience at the initial attempt may turn the individual away from it permanently. But it is also important in many other physical skills too. One of the advantages of modern educational gymnastics is that it avoids placing any individual in a distressing situation in the early days of learning gymnastic skills. Not only must upsetting experiences be avoided but also first impressions, since they affect motivation to a considerable extent, should as far as possible be happy ones. Thus in the initial stages of any skill learning, the child should have fun. The way in which a child will get fun and enjoyment from an activity will depend partly on his age and so the approach should be determined to a certain extent by this factor. If one makes a child repeat some skill such as a defensive forward stroke at cricket over and over again for a long period of time in order to get it grooved before he has appreciated the game and accepted the need for such practice the chances are that he will dislike cricket and give it up at the first opportunity.

The activity should be enjoyable and this enjoyment can be aided by success and praise.

Gebhard[55] conducted an experiment, with women subjects, into the effect of success and failure upon the attractiveness of activities and found that both past experience of success and expectation of future success were in general accompanied by a rise in attractiveness whereas experience of failure and expectation of failure were accompanied by a fall in attractiveness. Personal interest was also greater when success was experienced or expected. Sullivan[56] reported that 'in general, the time taken to learn a memory series is increased by the knowledge of failure in a previous performance and decreased by the knowledge of success in a previous performance' and that the women were more affected by reports of success and failure than were the men. Hurlock[57] showed in a study concerned with the learning of arithmetic by nine- and eleven-year-olds that the greatest amount of average improvement at the end of five days was found in the group which was publicly praised and encouraged. The 'reproved' group showed decidedly less improvement and the 'ignored' group less still. In accuracy the 'praised' group improved more than the 'reproved' group whereas the 'ignored' group showed a decrease. It was also shown that the girls were more affected than the boys and that reproof had a greater beneficial effect on the case of children judged by the initial test results to be the most able.

Public praise then improves performance but one may suspect that it might lose its value if used too often. In Hurlock's experiment reproof when first used was as valuable as praise but with continued use its effectiveness declined. Generalizations concerning the influence of punishment cannot safely be made. Punishment does work sometimes but there is no certainty what the effect will be. Often it causes a different reaction but not the desired one and sometimes it even appears to strengthen the wrong reaction.

Competition also improved performance both at the group level and even more at the individual level.[58] Since one learns what one practices it is very necessary to take part in competition if this is the way the activity is judged. Even in non-competitive forms of dance some rivalry may be a spur to perfection. Competition should however be used with care for, apart from the fact that it may cause antagonisms and other undesirable social attitudes with which this book is not concerned, it can sometimes impede skill acquisition in the long run. It may cause too much effort and attention to be put into winning at a particular level and not enough into the development of the skills needed to improve still further. A girl who can jump well using the scissors style may, if she engages continually in competition, never dare to change to another more mechanically efficient technique.

Again in a game like lawn tennis continuous competitive play leads a person gradually to leave out those strokes and tactics which are the biggest gamble and only to use those few strokes and tactical manœuvres which have been most developed and are therefore most reliable. But to continue to improve a tennis player should *add* to his repertoire of reliable strokes and tactics and frequently he will do this only if he practises strokes and plays games under non-competitive conditions or at least where he feels the results in terms of the score do not matter.

It is important for any learner clearly to understand the difference between playing any game for practice and playing to win. In the former the learner should try to use the appropriate technique or tactic irrespective of how well he can in fact carry it out whereas in the latter he should try to take advantage of his own strong points and leave out his weaknesses.

Unless a person is very highly motivated beneficial learning under competitive conditions is unlikely to take place if the learner knows he has no chance of winning. When groups of people of varying standard are learning together it is important that all should experience success for if a person continually fails he is likely to lose interest altogether. Not everyone wants to become an expert performer but most adolescents and adults want to feel they are improving. Success and failure are not absolute but relative to the learner's level of aspiration or goal and some kind of acknowledgement of merit rather than defeat should be available even to the poorest member of any group of learners.

Educational gymnastics, for instance, may enable all children in a class, even those who are relatively deficient in physical ability, to work at their own levels and so be successful at these levels. But whether particular children feel that they are successful or not will depend on their levels of aspiration. In the primary age group, the learner is usually energetic and inventive, and his goal tends to be immediate and unrelated to future attainment or to standards outside those of his own class or school. It is therefore relatively easy to interest him and to get him to explore his environment, to create new movements and to try out actions which are difficult for him. It may be more difficult however to get him to increase his control of those movements which he can already do for his span of attention is relatively short and he prefers to enjoy movement for its own sake rather than in terms of skill.

The older children however begin to want to do things well. They like a recognized ladder of achievement and they are more concerned with external standards. Motivating the children in educational gymnastics therefore becomes much more of a problem. There is a risk that the adolescent may spend his time repeating those actions which he can do, that he may not discover his own deficiencies or make any attempt to overcome them, and that he may not be able to make a true judgement either of his present abilities or of his potential. The more able pupils may lose interest because they cannot easily measure their improvement. In educational gymnastics then good teaching is necessary to ensure that the adolescent will increase his skill.

Any youngster can experience success if he is able to compete against his own record and is encouraged not to worry about his own standard relative to other peoples. In activities such as track and field athletics and swimming this is easy to do. In team games it is of course much more difficult. The use of tests for giving knowledge of results at, so to speak, lower levels than in the game itself not only helps an individual to find his own weaknesses as has already been suggested but also enables him to see how he is progressing. These signs of progress help to motivate him for knowledge of results encourages both self and social competition.

The Johnson[59] basket ball test for example consists of tests of shooting, of throwing accuracy and of dribbling the ball round hurdles, conducted under standardized conditions. It does not necessarily follow that a person who does well in tests will do well in a game, but testing provides incentives for some people and incidentally encourages practice in skills which are of use to the game.

Now it is necessary to consider the relative efficacy of certain other different methods of learning when used under constant conditions of motivation and teaching.

# IV

## FACTORS AFFECTING THE
## ACQUISITION OF SKILL (CONTINUED)

### (4) DISTRIBUTION OF PRACTICE

GIVEN A CERTAIN AMOUNT of time to spend on acquiring a skill, how should that time be spaced out? At one end there is the extreme case of practising continuously with no rest periods until the act has been acquired. With complex skills this is clearly impossible because of fatigue and because there is always room for improvement. Is it better then to have long or short practice periods and short or long rest periods?

Gross bodily skills require a minimal time for practice because of the need to 'warm-up' both in the physiological and psychological sense. Thus an individual who is trying to improve his high jump must get warmed-up so that his body is able to make the necessary movements without strain and he must also get mentally set or immersed in the activity so that he can give the skill his full attention. This minimal time will depend on the nature of the skill and also on the individual.

There is also a limit beyond which any practice period should not go. This will depend on the interest of the learner and on the fatigue engendered by the practice. But fatigue in this context does not depend solely on physical exertion. In some cases the limiting factor may be fatigue caused by physiological impairment of tissues but often the fatigue is of a more psychological nature. This fatigue may be expressed in subjective feelings of tiredness or boredom, or in an increase in the number of errors and periods of inattention. So far as skill acquisition is concerned it is useless to continue any practice once the individual ceases to be intensely interested in it. The maximum duration of a practice period, if it is to be beneficial, will therefore depend partially on the requirements of the skill but also to a great extent on the abilities and motivation of the individual learner. Many skilled performers set themselves a training schedule and go through with it at all costs. From the point of view of skill acquisition the evidence is that this is wrong though it may help to build up other necessary qualities such as strength and stamina. For example, if one is practising the smash at tennis, so long as one is improving or maintaining one's standard it is worth continuing the practice but as soon as the skill begins to break down it is important from the point of view of skill improvement either to stop practising the smash or to put in some new challenges to raise one's interest again. Similarly, the number of practices of the vault which a pole-vaulter can usefully do on any one occasion is limited and, therefore, in this sort of activity, progress in skill must be slow. Some skills take a long time to acquire for this reason.

The period which can usefully be spent on a skill at any practice time is therefore limited. Practice is exhausting for the beginner because he tenses many unnecessary muscles and dissipates much nervous energy. The optimum period of practice for him will therefore usually be less than that for the good performer. The adult beginner can practise usefully for a longer period than a young child provided the motivation is the same, for his powers of concentration are greater. The more strongly motivated an individual the longer he can apply the necessary intense effort and attention. Individuals vary tremendously in their ability to sustain concentration on any particular practice. The teacher can help by encouragement, providing new ideas and setting goals just ahead of the learner and within reach of his attainment in a fairly short time.

Within the two limits of the minimum and maximum it may be theorized that there is an optimal length of practice for a particular person learning a particular skill.

Travis[60] for example found indications that for the manual pursuit oscillator 4-minute practice sessions were inferior to 2-minute lengths when the inter-practice rests were constant at 3-minutes. He points out that much of the practice in the 4-minute period was a 'waste of time and actually deleterious to learning of this type'. In the field of gross bodily skills controlled investigations into the length of practice period alone do not appear to have been carried out. Experiments where the length of rest was also varied have been reported by Knapp *et al.*[61] They found that, in learning to juggle 3 balls, groups of American high school boys and college students learned more quickly if they practised 5 minutes every day than if they tried for 15 minutes every other day. One minute of practice in the shorter session was worth 1·78 minutes and 1·8 minutes in the longer with boys and students respectively. The significance of the difference was at the 1 per cent level of confidence. It is interesting to note too that a higher number of those in the 15-minute group failed to reach the criterion of 100 consecutive catches than in the 5-minute group. Little and often seemed then to be the best method.

Other studies concerned solely with the length of rest period have produced inconclusive results. Cozens[62] offered evidence that 'with the 100-yard dash, 120-yard low hurdles, half-mile run, running broad jump, 12-lb. shot and discus throw, improvement is more marked when the practice periods are spread over a considerable period of time rather than concentrated'. This, he said, might lead to the conclusion that for track athletes 3 periods per week of 1 hour spread over a year is better than periods of 1 hour per day for 6 days a week for half a year. Scott[63] found some indication that for beginners learning to swim four half-hour periods per week were more satisfactory than either two half-hour periods or two 50-minute periods per week. The numbers in the groups were very small however and results were not statistically significant. Young[64] suggested that in archery 4 days per week seemed to result in more rapid learning than a 2-day per week distribution, whereas in badminton where progress was measured by three skill tests the reverse appeared true. When trying to explain the difference in her results Young mentions that other experimenters have found that learning in the early stages seems to be improved when the practice periods are relatively massed but that once fundamental learning has taken place, learning is more rapid if the practices are distributed over longer periods of time. Thus, to her students, archery was an entirely new type of skill whereas experience in other racket games might have affected their learning of badminton.

Intensive swimming schemes have been put into practice in several parts of England. In Ilford junior schools for instance the third-year class (nine- and 10-year-olds) have 20 minutes' swimming instruction each school day for a period of three consecutive weeks.

Between November 1959 and July 1960, approximately 65 per cent of those who could not swim a width at the beginning of the course could do so by the end of it.[65]

Lashley[66] has suggested that two stages in learning should be distinguished: the stage of exploration and adjustment during which the right response is discovered, and the stage of fixation during which the right response is made more certain. But among psychologists there are differences of opinion on whether relative massing of the practice time helps the stage of exploration or not. On the whole the later work puts forward the view that massing leads to more variability of response and, in a complex skill, is therefore beneficial in the early stage because it makes the chance of hitting on the right response more likely. However, when a good response has been found, then distribution of practice tends to produce the required 'fixation' in less total practice time.

If this is true then it would seem that when a new skill is to be acquired, practice periods should be very frequent but that once a good response has been discovered, the practice periods can be interspersed with longer rest periods. An experiment[67] into the learning of billiards seems to support this view. It was found that a group who had their practice sessions on what was called the additive basis obtained significantly better results with the same total amount of practice than three other groups with various practice distributions. The group on the additive basis had practice on days 1, 2, 3, 5, 8, 13, 21, 34 and 55. In effect this is relative massing at the beginning and widely spaced time intervals at the end. Of the other three groups one had daily practice for nine days running, one had practice on the Monday, Tuesday and Wednesday of each week and one had practice once per week. No significant difference was found between these three groups.

One advantage of spaced practice is that it gives a chance for some of the less beneficial movements built up during learning to dissipate during the rest pauses. It is an advantage to forget some of the things one has done! Bartlett[68] commented that 'in order that any complex series of bodily movements should be given a fair chance to be consolidated, or organized, very persistent and prolonged repetition should be avoided'. It has been found frequently that performance may reach new

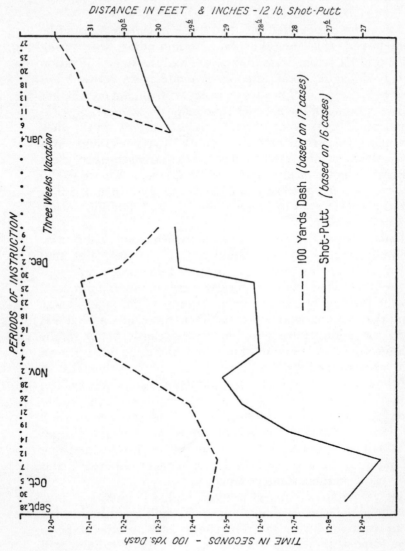

Fig. 7. Learning curves. From F. W. Cozens, 1933.

heights after a period of no practice. It will be seen that this must have occurred in some of the cases used to make the curve of learning for the shot-putt in Fig. 7. A striking example known to the author was of a beginner who after ten weeks' intensive effort could not swim at all but who on his return to the bath after three weeks' Christmas holiday swam a width.

The effect of any period of no practice will of course depend to a certain extent upon what is done during it. Thus, as has already been pointed out, improvement may occur if the period is one in which motor activity is minimal, provided a fair amount of practice has been put in in the first place. If on the other hand a person practises some other physical activity during the interval this may interfere with his performance. Then again if he spends some of the time during the period of rest thinking about the activity he may find an improvement over and above that which would have occurred with rest alone. Mental practice has been shown to be effective in tossing rope-rings ten feet on to a wooden peg, throwing darts, throwing balls at a target, and making basketball free throws. Some results are given in Table 2. It is interesting to note that in Clark's experiment the more experienced boys made almost as great an improvement with mental practice as with physical whereas the novice groups did not. Apparently 'a certain amount of motor experience is necessary before mental practice will provide a maximal effect'.

During learning the periods of no practice must not be so long that too much is forgotten and the over-all time must also be borne in mind. If a student must learn some skill during a course which is limited in length it may be necessary to have relative massing of practices even though each minute spent in actual practice results in less than optimal learning. In real life of course the picture is often confused by the fact that people who mass their practices also usually put in a greater total time.

Before this section is summarized it might be advisable to consider 'pressure training'. This is a method of intensifying training during a particular period of time. In tennis or football for instance a player may be put under extreme pressure by being made to deal in a particular way with a much more rapid sequence of balls than would normally occur in the game itself.

TABLE 2

| No. of subjects in each Group | No. of days of experiment | Time spent in mental practice by Group 2 | No. of throws per day physical practice of Groups 3 | Per cent improvement | | |
|---|---|---|---|---|---|---|
| | | | | Control (Group 1) | Mental Practice (Group 2) | Physical Practice (Group 3) |
| *Dart-throwing* (1) | | | | | | |
| 4 Junior H.S. Boys | 20 | 30 mins. daily | 25 | −2 | 4 | 7 |
| 4 College men | 20 | 30 mins. daily | 25 | 0 | 22 | 23 |
| *Basketball free throws* (1) | | | | | | |
| 4 Senior H.S. Boys | 20 | 15 mins. daily | 35 | 2 | 43 | 41 |
| *Ring-tossing* (2) | | | | | | |
| 12 College men | 22 | 15 mins. daily | 70 | 4·3 | 36·2 | 137·3 |
| *Throwing balls at a target* (3) | | | | | | |
| 15 English schoolboys 14 yrs. approx. | 10 | 10 mins. daily | 25 | 7·56 | 11·90 | 15·32 |
| *Pacific Coast one-hand foul shot* (4) | | | | | | |
| 48 H.S. Boys (a) Varsity | 14 | Imagined shooting 30 each day | 30 | No control group | 15 | 16 |
| (b) Junior Varsity | 14 | ditto | 30 | ditto | 23 | 24 |
| (c) Novice | 14 | ditto | 30 | ditto | 26 | 44 |

(1) Vandell, Davis and Clugston (1943). *J. Gen. P.*, Vol. 29, pp. 243–50.

(2) Twining (1949). These subjects were not equated as to ability to learn gross bodily motor skills nor as to general motor ability. *R. Q.*, Vol. 20, pp. 432–5.

(3) Steel (1952). *J. of P. E.*, Vol. 44, pp. 101–8.

(4) Clark (1960). *R. Q.*, Vol. 31, pp. 560–59.

Note that the amount of practice under the two conditions physical and mental was not truly equated. An attempt was made to do this by Clark but the mental practice subjects also read each time a written introduction to the mental practice technique.

Winterbottom[69] has given some examples of pressure practices in football. For instance, he talks about teaching the skill of heading by pressure training. 'The centre forward (A) is being coached to deflect goalwards a ball that drops level with the near post but some distance from goal. He runs to A1 and jumps to head the ball over to the far corner of the goal. He then runs to A2 to head the ball to the opposite side of goal. Then back to A1 and so on' (Fig. 8).

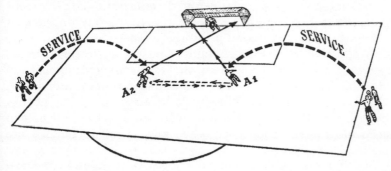

FIG. 8. Pressure training. From W. Winterbottom, 1957.

Similarly in tennis one person at the net volleys balls which are driven at him alternately by two players. The one player drives his ball just as the person at net volleys the one before. Winterbottom points out that pressure training may also be applied to tactical practices. Thus the defence in football may be subject to waves of attack from two different attacking groups, the second group beginning its attack each time the group before has either scored or the ball has been cleared over the half-way line.

Pressure training appears to have certain advantages and certain limitations. In the first place, when a skilled movement has been learned at leisure then pressure training may quicken it up by making the learner or learners cut out unnecessary movements and react to the more important and earlier cues. Secondly, when an individual has acquired many skilled movements his actual level of skill in a game or sport may be determined by his ability to select the best method of dealing with the situation from among many actions which would all be appropriate to some degree. Pressure-training may aid this selection. Crossman[70] in considering a manual speed-skill suggests that its acquisition depends primarily on a selective process. 'The trainer must first know what is to be selected, i.e. what methods (both perceptual and motor) give fast performance; secondly, he must ensure that the learner can do them; and thirdly he must set up conditions in which they are consistently more successful than all others.

'Verbal or visual instruction and demonstration are of use for putting the best methods into the repertoire, but for selection systematic practice under pressure for speed is probably the only effective way.' Practice under pressure applies then to the selection, to meet changes in the external environment, of movements which are already in the repertoire of the individual.

Thirdly, pressure training may be used to make the experienced performer realize that with an effort of will he can keep his skill in action even when all sorts of discomforts are claiming his attention. By recognizing the symptoms and effects of fatigue he can learn to cope with them and can learn to perform the skill under trying and distracting conditions. Under these circumstances the skill itself may change but so long as the intended end result is achieved then pressure training may be considered to be advantageous. But pressure training should be stopped if the skill does actually break down because otherwise the learner may be destroying the skill he has already acquired. Pressure training is then of no use in the early stages of acquiring skill for 'the method adopted when fatigued will seldom be as efficient as the method adopted when not'.[71] But in so far as it intensifies effort and concentrates attention on the task in hand it can be useful to the more advanced performer. However it should not be continued when the skill begins to break down – unless of course one is trying to break it down in order to build up an entirely new one.

As a summary it may be said that, from the point of view of skill learning, a short period of intense effort and attention is better than a half-hearted longer period. Quality of practice rather than quantity is required. At the beginning frequent periods of shortish length seem advisable but when the foundations have been laid practices can be longer and less frequent. Mental practice during periods of no physical activity can be beneficial. What is a reasonable period of practice will depend on the activity and on the powers of concentration and the interest of the learner. The practice period must be long enough to enable the individual to get warmed up. But it must not be so long that fatigue sets in. In general, practice should be stopped when fatigue or loss of interest is beginning to introduce errors, when good responses are beginning to break up and bad habits are being formed. Goodenough and Brian[72] have summed up in the statement that the 'greatest efficiency may perhaps be gained by appropriate interruption of practice at times when the setting up of undesirable habits seems to be retarding progress'.

## (5) SPEED AND ACCURACY

It has been suggested that, in teaching a skill where both speed and accuracy are required, it is better to retard the speed of movement in the early stages of practice until a high degree of accuracy is reached and then gradually to increase speed. (Poppelreuters 'law'). This is based on the assumption that it is easier to speed up accurate movements than to correct fast inaccurate ones.

Others[73] have pointed out that this implies that increase of speed is merely a matter of gradually increasing the tempo while the movement remains the same and that this implication is not true. A slow movement is performed differently from a fast one even though the path of the movement is not changed. As a result of experimentation Sperry[74] has written that 'changes in speed . . . cause extreme variations in the physiological patterns underlying what, from an unanalytical observation, might appear to be a fairly constant simple response'.

It would seem from this that where speed is vital to performance, speed is a part of form and should therefore be emphasized from the beginning. This would particularly appear to be so where the part of the body which is moving fast is free from muscular tension in the middle of its course and is carried on by its own momentum. Hartson[75] has stated that 'since the individual ballistic movement cannot be made slowly, it must be speeded from the outset'. A ballistic movement is one in which the contraction of the positive muscle group relaxes long before

55

the end of the movement so that there is a momentum phase free of muscular action. The following actions have been included by various writers under this term: the football kick, the pitch in baseball, rapid walking and running, swimming, rowing, throwing, handling the steering wheel of a boat, diving, golf and tennis strokes. Slater-Hammel[76] has however produced some evidence to show that the tennis forehand drive is of the non-ballistic type.

Of course, even where a ballistic movement is present, other types of movement will also be involved. For example, rapid walking and running consist of ballistic thrusts of the legs while the upright posture is held by moving fixations of the trunk.

In skills then where speed is all-important, like javelin and discus throwing, swimming, the sprint start, the evidence is strongly in favour of early emphasis on speed. Clearly the learner cannot be expected to perform at the speed of the skilled person for he has to exercise more conscious control, has difficulty in selecting the more important external and internal signals and in differentiating between the necessary and unnecessary muscular contractions, and he lacks the ability to anticipate. Nevertheless he should aim for speed.

Now, however, skills must be considered where accuracy of aim is as important as speed. What effect will emphasis on speed have on accuracy?

Fulton[77] found no significant difference in accuracy or speed between two groups who learned to hit a ball 'backhand' with bat across the line of the ball. One group aimed at speed throughout and the other was instructed to try to make sure to contact the ball and only increase the speed of the swing when their accuracy was high. At the end there was a difference in the distribution of the speed within the stroke. The 'accuracy' group had a more uniform distribution whereas the 'speed' group showed a definite gain of momentum in the middle of the stroke. Fulton[78] then carried out further experiments involving a striking movement and a tracing movement and found that accuracy was an 'unstable factor which was fairly specific to the practised speed. Training for accuracy at slow speeds had little advantage at higher speeds' in the case of ballistic or non-ballistic skills. In the post-training period for the ballistic skill when speed and accuracy was the aim almost all the accuracy gained at a low speed was lost. Although the accuracy group was still the more accurate at the end of the experiment the difference was not significant. In the case of the non-ballistic skill however, throughout the post-training period the superiority of the accuracy group in accuracy and the speed group in speed was significant. It was noticed that the methods of accomplishing the skill differed between the two groups. In both experiments the speed-set transferrred to the speed-accuracy situation. To put it another way a person who had been trained to do the act at speed, when required to be accurate, did not lose his speed to any great extent. The experiment showed that early emphasis on speed did not necessarily result in the establishment of 'habits of inaccuracy' and that where accumulation of momentum is essential, early emphasis on speed is even more justified. Unfortunately these experiments were very short term involving only twenty-two and twenty-six trials respectively.

Solley[79] had three groups of students, thirty-five or more in each group, learn a motor skill in which the subject stepped forward over a distance equal to his height and struck a fixed target. During the first half of the experiment one of the groups was instructed verbally to emphasize speed, another accuracy and another speed and accuracy equally. During the second half all groups were told to give equal emphasis to speed and accuracy. The experiment lasted six weeks and 180 thrusts were made by each subject.

Solley concluded from his results that speed developed under initial emphasis of speed readily transferred into performance where both speed and accuracy were considered important and the transfer was very persistent. Accuracy gained at low rates of speed was lost almost immediately when the rate of performance was increased. The tenor of these conclusions agrees with Fulton. But Solley also pointed out that all three groups were approaching equal levels of speed and accuracy at the end of the experiment and so he goes on to suggest that Poppelreuter's law should be altered to read:

(a) In skills in which speed is the predominate factor for successful performance the most efficient results are obtained by early emphasis of speed.

(b) In skills in which both speed and accuracy are important to successful performance, emphasis on both speed and accuracy yields the most desirable results.

The statement (a) agrees with what has already been said earlier and (b) suggest that in skills such as striking or throwing as they occur in team games, racket games, fencing, or boxing, the emphasis should be on both speed and accuracy.

This question of speed and accuracy is a very important one and the evidence to date cannot be considered conclusive or entirely clear. It does however appear that where a skill requires the accumulation of momentum it should be learned at such a speed that a ballistic-type movement is produced from the first. Even when this is done however there will still be a choice of speed, for ballistic skills are also capable of speed variation.

Aiming for speed then does not necessarily mean that a learner should attempt the greatest speed of hit or kick or other striking action from the beginning. In team and racket games for example many different skill speeds are required in the truly skilled performer and accuracy at each speed level will have to be learned. The top-class performers at football and hockey must be able to send the balls short as well as long distances; the tennis player must be able to alter the speed of the ball and hit the ball relatively softly as well as very hard. Should one then learn initially the slower movements – though still fast in the sense that they are not modifiable at the time and are often ballistic in nature – or attempt the highest speeds? Even a ballistic movement is capable of delicate adjustment in extent and force. Since any error which is made will be increased by the application of greater force and since tactical considerations are one of the major contributions to the enjoyment of games, it seems likely that learners should be taught the slower speeds at first but that these speeds should be fast enough for the movements to be useful ones to the skilled player. The learner can then be accurate enough to take part in games which, although played at a relatively slow speed, can nevertheless give opportunities for tactics and team co-operation to be learned. Faster accurate movements can then be acquired gradually and even if the maximal speed of hit or kick is never successfully acquired the performers will be really playing the game and appreciating the tactical side. In tennis an individual who always tries to hit as hard as a Wimbledon champion is likely to have no rallies for he will occasionally hit a winner but more often a stream of losers. Riggs[80], former Wimbledon champion, has said 'When learning any shot, start off by playing steadily and

try all the time to make the shot correctly. When the fundamentals have been mastered, say after three or four years, you
can start speeding up. Steadiness and the cultivation of soundness first and speed afterwards is standard teaching in America
and a system which has produced such players as Kramer,
Budge, Schroeder, Mulloy, Parker and myself to name but a
few cannot be too bad.'

## (6) WHOLE AND PART LEARNING

In the whole method material is learned by going through it
completely time after time. In the part method the material is
divided into portions and these are practised and then connected with each other. The part method can be subdivided
according to the way in which the parts are subsequently connected with each other. For example each part may be learned
separately to a criterion and then an attempt can be made to
join them all together. Sometimes however each part is learned
on its own but parts 1 and 2 are put together before part 3 is
mastered; and then again parts 1, 2 and 3 are practised together
before part 4 is learned and so on. Sometimes again part 1 is
learned, then parts 1 and 2 together, then parts 1, 2 and 3 so
that in effect part 1 is repeated most times. Sometimes in motor
skills the parts are not learned in the order in which they are
performed in the final skill. For instance in discus throwing one
might learn the final part of the throwing action before practising the turn.

Then there is a third way to be considered. This is termed the
whole-part-whole method. In this the learner tries to do the
whole act from time to time and then practises parts of the act,
particularly those parts which he finds most difficult.

Psychologists are very wary of making any generalizations
on this matter. Bugelski[81] has gone so far as to say that 'the
whole method, when it applies at all, is restricted to the learning of rote memory material, the learning of poetry, and similar
activities. It has little relevance outside of this province and
burdening teachers with advice about it seems largely wasteful'.
Others point out the difficulty of deciding in any particular context exactly what a whole or part is. In spite of these comments

a great deal of experimentation has been carried out and much of it has been concerned with the learning of fine motor skills. There is evidence in favour of various methods and no one method seems conclusively the best for every skill. In fact even for one particular skill the best method is often dependent to a certain extent on the individual learner. Although it is difficult to come to any general conclusions the matter is such an important one that it must be discussed.

There have been some experiments into the gross bodily skills and it is desirable to look first at the results from them. Shay[82] equated, on the basis of motor ability and physical capacity, thirty-two men who had no previous experience on any piece of gymnastic apparatus. Group A was then taught the upstart or kip on the horizontal bar by attempting the entire exercise at each trial or, in other words, by the whole method of learning. Group B worked with a part procedure in which they first learned the swing and after it had been mastered the arch of the body during the swing was added. After this combined exercise had been learned, the flexion of the thighs bringing the feet to the bar was given. After these three movements had been satisfactorily completed the extension of the thighs was added, resulting in a position of front rest on the horizontal bar.

The goal was shown to each group at the beginning and the experiment was carefully explained. The subjects were taught in classes of eight in order to help hold their interest throughout the experiment. The same number of trials was given to each man during each class period and at the end the horizontal bar was taken down so that there would not be any uncontrolled practice. The criterion of success at this skill was the ability to perform the upstart three consecutive times. The results are given in Table 3.

TABLE 3

|  | Group A (Whole method) | Group B (Part Method) |
|---|---|---|
| Total number of trials | 616 | 781 |
| Mean | 38·5 | 48·8 |
| Standard deviation | 9·80 | 8·04 |

$$\frac{D}{\sigma \text{ diff.}} = 3\cdot3$$

The difference between the means is significant at the 1 per cent level of confidence and it may therefore be concluded that it is better to teach students the upstart by the whole method rather than by this type of part method.

Wickstrom[83] compared the whole method with the whole direct repetitive method for teaching ten basic gymnastic skills to male students. In the latter method the skill was demonstrated and described in detail twice so that the subjects understood the nature of the whole activity. They were then taught by the part method in which part 1 is learned, then parts 1 and 2 together and so on. In two of the skills however the last part was practised separately before being added. The results were not clear-cut but the evidence was mainly in favour of the whole method. Only in one case however was the difference statistically significant.

In an experiment[84] into learning to juggle three balls the trend favoured the whole approach. For teaching boys and girls aged seven-and-a-half to nine-and-a-half years to swim Niemeyer[85] reports that Lewellen found a whole method superior to a part method. Niemeyer also states that 'Combs concluded the part method was superior in teaching selected track events' but that 'the only complete track activity was the shot-put, and in this event the whole group was superior'. He points out that the students in the whole method group were not given any instruction beyond an initial demonstration whereas the others received instruction continuously.

Niemeyer himself conducted experiments with male students in regular physical education classes on the relative effectiveness over a period of nine to ten weeks of whole and part methods of learning swimming, badminton and volley ball. Both groups in each activity received instruction, the fundamental difference between the groups being that the whole method group never practised parts though parts were demonstrated and explained to them. In the case of swimming Niemeyer found that the students in the whole method group learned to swim sooner, farther and faster and showed better form.

If games are now considered it is found that there is very little experimental evidence and most of what there is can be strongly criticized for one reason or another. Three separate investigations into basket-ball concluded that a part method procedure was superior to a whole method. Of these, Hause's[86] experiment was with very small groups and only dealt with shooting, and Kimball's was carried out in such a way that the whole method group received no instruction and was tested on parts whereas the part method group was taught and tested on parts. The third investigation, which was carried out by Cross[88] was with fifteen-year-old boys and found that the whole method was more effective in teaching simple unitary functions like passing and catching but that the whole-part-whole method was better for some of more complex skills. The serious weakness in this study was that the whole method group was not given instruction. Performance results obtained by Niemeyer[89] in volleyball indicated that the part method was significantly better than the whole method whereas those in badminton indicated that there was nothing to choose between the two methods. But performance results were measured by means of the Brady Volleyball Test and the Miller Wall Test of Badminton respectively. Although both tests have been validated by using test results against total playing ability (Brady ·86, Miller ·83) this is not an entirely satisfactory method of testing performance in a game. This point and also the fact that no long-term experiments have been conducted make conclusions difficult.

It seems then that so far as individual-type activities, in which the performer acts on his own, are concerned the evidence, though not conclusive, is predominantly in favour of the whole method for beginners. So far as games are concerned the evidence is scanty and unsatisfactory but what there is indicates that some form of part method *may* be better. In this connexion it is of interest that Cross[90] comments 'probably the practice of the parts proved most valuable as much because of the simplifying of the intellectual concepts, as because of the simplifying of the motor co-ordination'. Rodgers[91] has pointed out that no attempt should be made to teach 'part-game' skills until students have been exposed to the whole game and recognize the need for these skills. In teaching practice many different methods and combinations of method are used.

What are the factors which may affect the efficacy of any particular method? Two important factors are motivation and type of skill.

*Motivation*

When a person learns a complex skill by the whole method it may take quite a long time before any beneficial results become apparent to the learner. He may have to put in a great deal of effort before he makes any progress judged by measurable results. Unless motivation is strong he may therefore give up before he acquires the skill. Once measurable progress begins it is likely to be steadier and less subject to plateaux than if the part method is used.

On the other hand the parts are easier to learn than the whole and so, if the part method is used, the learner appears to be making more progress and so he is happier and enjoys the practice more. He has many intermediary targets which he can attain and these will encourage him to continue his efforts. But human beings only learn what they practise and so it may well take the learner longer in the end to learn the whole for only some of the skill and knowledge gained in learning the parts will be transferred. The whole is a quite unique action with its own particular attributes. The acquisition of the whole is therefore not just a case of fitting the parts together and a great deal more time and effort may be required before the final end is achieved. This is particularly likely to be so if the learner has not been given a good idea of the whole at the beginning of his practice.

There are certain serious difficulties in the use of the part method. In the first place a plateau of learning often occurs at the time the parts are being joined together and if these plateaux occur too frequently the learner may get despondent and give up. Secondly, even when the whole skill has been acquired, a weakness may be left in the skill at the place where the parts are joined. For instance, in learning the discus throw, if the turn and throw are learned separately, then the timing of the whole act may never become satisfactory. Again in the javelin throw great difficulty may be experienced in trying to get the power from the run-up translated into the speed of the javelin. Thirdly there is the difficulty in deciding what should be taken as a 'part' in any particular skill. Clearly the part must be viewed in its context, for if the over-all rhythm or basic pattern of the movement is destroyed the part method will prove disadvantageous. For instance, hurdling is in essence a running event over a number of obstacles. Therefore in learning it is better to run over several hurdles however low they have to be rather than to perfect technique over one hurdle at the proper height. This point raises the question therefore of the skill itself.

## Type of Skill

First the method is likely to depend to a certain extent on the complexity of the skill. There is probably an upper limit to the amount of material that any given learner can grasp as a unit and a lower limit below which subdivision into parts is not only unnecessary but also wasteful of time and effort. No person who can grasp a later stage in the part-whole process and whose aim is to learn the whole skill should be made to begin at an earlier stage. The problem must therefore be solved to a certain extent in terms of the learner's abilities and motivation. Some individuals seem to prefer the part method while others appear to learn better by the whole. Young children can get a great deal of fun in acquiring the parts. Indeed what constitutes a part for the adult may be a whole for a child with his limited grasp of meaning. A child of eight may play something which he calls football but because he cannot understand team co-operation the whole will not be the same as for the adolescent.

The whole method is then probably the best when the skill can be acquired to a moderate level of performance fairly quickly and when the skill is a relatively simple one for the learner. Examples might be throwing, catching and striking a ball, somersaulting or climbing a rope. When however the skill is a relatively complex one like throwing the javelin, pole-vaulting, playing the major team or racket games, it may be better to use the part method.

So far as complex skills are concerned however the question must be examined further. The first point to be considered is the speed of the skill. It has been pointed out previously that a fast movement should not be learned at a slow rate because the movement itself is thereby altered. There is also a period of time during which a voluntary correction cannot be made. This is the time taken for impulses to be conducted to the brain from the sense organs, for a decision to be made and for the motor impulses to be carried to the muscles. It has been estimated for instance that 'a rapid aiming movement which is completed in about ·5 seconds cannot contain a voluntary correction'.[92] It follows from these two points that no attempt should be made to divide very fast movements into parts. Presumably where a skill such as the javelin throw involves a series of fast movements over a longer period of time a division can be made but this point should nevertheless be borne in mind.

The second point to consider is the way in which the parts are related to the whole motor action. Thus the parts may be ones which are performed simultaneously in the whole skill or they may be ones which occur in succession. Examples of the first are the leg and arm movements in the crawl stroke, and the act of putting the ball in the air and swinging the racket in the tennis service. Examples of the latter in which the parts occur in succession are the sprint start and the hurdling action in hurdling one hundred and twenty yards, the discus turn and throw, the javelin run and throw and the pole-vault.

When the parts are performed simultaneously the part method is less desirable because the act of putting the parts together to form the whole is a much greater problem and is likely to cause a plateau of relatively long duration. It must always be remembered that man operates as an organism and that all parts of his body are therefore interdependent. Davis[93] for instance has shown that there is muscular activity in all four limbs when a voluntary movement of one extremity is made. Sperry[94] too has pointed out that there are 'elaborate modifications in the neuro-muscular co-ordination of a given movement when the rate of the movement is varied and when the supporting postures are modified'. To the observer, movement patterns producing the same end-result may appear identical but in fact the constituent co-ordinations may be quite different because of differing postural adjustments or other variations within the individual. It *may* be necessary because of the conditions under which swimming has to be learned in public baths in England to resort to part methods in order to build up the learner's confidence. It would probably be preferable however to learn by the whole method in much shallower water. Again in tennis provided the learner can throw and generally control a ball, the serving action is better taught by the whole method (see Plates 2 and 7).

When however the action is a fairly lengthy one in which the parts occur in succession then the whole-part-whole method can be helpful. This is because each subsequent part of the act depends on the accuracy of the one before. Thus in performing the javelin throw the run must be performed consistently so that the mainly internal cues for the last part of the action are highly similar. In the case of a competitive hurdler too it would be useless to be able to do the hurdling action well if the start could not be made in such a way as to arrive consistently in the same appropriate spot for the first hurdle.

The discussion so far has been concerned mainly with the motor action in which the internal signals from the proprioceptive system are largely concerned. Skill in activities like diving, Olympic gymnastics, swimming and athletics depends to a very large extent on the efficiency of the techniques and changes in the external environment play a relatively small part. On the other hand in team and racket games the motor action must be an appropriate one to deal with the environmental cues and so perception of the needs of the situation becomes extremely important. To put it another way, the expert in the former activities must possess the motor co-ordination of the skill almost to perfection whereas in a game the player is unlikely to possess all the possible personal techniques and only a few of those he has will he have perfected to a very high level. He must however be able to use those techniques which he does possess to the best advantage and it is the ability to take into account the weaknesses and strengths of the opposing side, the members of his own team and himself and to make the right judgement in any particular situation which stamps him as a skilled performer.

In these skills then the signals from the external environment play a vital part. In cricket the batsman must make the right judgement about the approaching ball before the motor action of the stroke becomes important. A beautifully executed stroke based on a wrong judgement may have a disastrous result. As Bartlett[95] puts it 'the skilled performer must know more *what* to do than *how* to do it'. To enable him to do this the skilled performer picks up the information which enables him to act to his advantage very much earlier than the unskilled. When any particular action is being taken by an opponent or a team-mate a series of incoming signals are received, and the more skilled the performer the more he takes notice of the signals which are early in the series. In an invariant sequence the later signals are redundant to him. For example, once the bowler has released the ball and probably even a little before this time its path has been determined. The skilled player can pick up these cues whereas the unskilled person waits for much

66

later cues in the series and therefore does not act until the ball has almost arrived. He is trying to carry out a stroke under difficult if not impossible conditions and incidentally under conditions which will not arise when he is more skilled at 'reading the signs'. In fact he may learn a stroke which will be quite inappropriate when he is skilled.

In this case then it seems desirable to spend a considerable amount of time on the perceptual aspects of such skills and particularly on identifying the cues which the expert uses so that the learner can be helped to identify the relevant signals and appreciate their relative importance. But in many games the external signals are themselves directly influenced by the responses that the player makes and so the inexpert performer creates more problems for himself or his team-mates. For example, a player of any racket game who cannot execute a stroke well enough to put the ball or shuttle within a reasonable distance of his target creates a great many difficulties for himself so far as the next stroke is concerned. If his variability on one stroke is very great he presents himself with an almost impossible situation on the next and what is more important it is a situation with which he will not normally have to deal when he can make his own stroke more accurately. Thus the skilful racket player is performing the easier task for he knows where his opponent will be when he strikes the ball and he knows also the probable and possible strokes from that position. But as Annett and Kay[96] have said 'until responses achieve some measure of consistency the operator may well be trying to learn a task which is of his own designing and bears only occasional relationship to the task in hand'. They suggest that part learning is best in a task where the learner's responses substantially affect the cues he will receive from the external environment. This presumably also applies where the responses are affecting the cues not only of himself but also of his team-mates as in football or hockey. But it should be noted that the 'part' referred to is not a division of the motor action but of the whole activity. This supports the traditional practice of tennis coaches who feed a learner with a continuous series of balls to the same place and at the same speed so that he may learn to hit the ball back consistently to a predetermined spot on the court. There is, however, a danger in it if it is continued for too long because it is not possible to learn to deal with difficult situations by practising in easy ones (see Plate 8).

Seymour[97] has made certain observations which are relevant here. He has pointed out that 'many industrial tasks involve no fixed "whole" but the operators' skills consist largely in the ability to do, on demand, any one of a number of possible combinations of parts'. The same comment could be applied to tasks which arise in games. He has also suggested that 'the terms "part" and "whole" are misleading and inadequate' and that it might be desirable to talk instead 'of "isolation" methods of training for difficult industrial tasks'. This idea of 'isolation' is an interesting one. Skills in physical education and recreation are wholes. They are not made up of separate parts in the sense that one can define the parts, teach any individual those parts and expect him, by joining the parts together, to produce the whole. In other words the whole is not the sum of the parts. Except therefore in the case of a dangerous activity (and even here if harness or other support can be used) the learner should first have a go at the whole skill. But in the practice of the whole, unless it is a simple skill, there will be parts which are more difficult for the particular individual to acquire. These parts which may be isolated for practice, will not be the same for each individual for they are not structural to the skill but only more difficult for the particular learner to acquire. Not only can action patterns or parts of action patterns be isolated but also situations as when learning a particular tactical move between half-back and two forwards in association football or the combination of the pack in a tight scrum at rugby football.

It is therefore necessary to try the whole and then isolate the parts for practice according to each individual's or team's difficulties. These difficulties may be concerned with the motor side or, more probably in team and racket games, with the perceptual aspects. The fact that the time required for a movement in the latter activities depends on its perceptual as well as its spatial characteristics has not been sufficiently recognized and too little time has therefore been spent on this 'part' of skill. Indeed not enough is known about the cues to which the skilled player reacts and investigation in this sphere for any particular game would be invaluable. This idea of isolation means that the teacher will not have any fixed parts in his mind nor will he make any individual practice any 'part' unless he is having difficulty with it. Indeed it would be unhelpful even to draw attention to a possible difficulty if the individual has not come up against it himself. Of course, when a class is being dealt with and several of the pupils have the same difficulty, it may appear to a casual observer that the part-whole method is being used since a group can be separated out for a particular practice. But the approach to the problem is quite different.

It is possible then to sum up this very difficult question of whole and part learning by saying that until such time as detailed experimental evidence concerning each skill is produced, it is probably best in the learning of skills in physical education and physical recreation to start with the whole method while feeling free to concentrate at any time in the case of a particular individual on any part where there is some difficulty or weakness impeding the production and perfecting of the whole skill.

# V

## FACTORS WHICH VARY WITH
## THE LEARNER

IN THE LAST two chapters different methods of learning skills were examined. These methods can be controlled and manipulated independently of the learner, and their general effects have been discussed. It was assumed that every individual had the necessary physical and mental attributes and wanted to acquire the skill. In the experiments the individuals in the control and experimental groups were usually equated in some way so that the effects of particular methods of learning could be distinguished. But in practice when any particular method is used the results vary from individual to individual. It is now necessary therefore to consider those variables which are direct characteristics of the learner.

These variables may affect the speed with which a given level of performance is reached not only by their influence on the rate of learning but also by their effect on initial ability. It can be seen by reference to figures 3, 4, 5 and 6 that initial ability is often above zero. Thus two complete beginners at squash rackets or throwing the javelin may learn at the same rate but one may reach a set standard of skill in less time because his initial level of ability was higher. Initial ability is compounded from many variables including age, inherited characteristics and previous experience.

## (1) AGE

It is apparent that a child must be old enough to learn a particular activity before practice will have any beneficial effect. A child cannot be taught to run races before he can walk nor can a six-year-old child learn to play a team game like football or hockey. Johnny was given special training in riding a tricycle but he failed to learn before the age when most children do.[98] Being old enough is determined not by chronological age but by physiological age, by the stage of maturation reached by the learner. Maturation may be defined as the physiological ripening of an organism and refers to that part of the development towards mature size and condition which results from causes other than specific activity or functioning. Maturation therefore in no way depends on exercise. Although there can be few acts in an adult which are wholly unlearned it is important to understand the contribution of maturation. There are no wholly learned acts because the structures which enable performance to take place are laid down in the rough by maturation.

It is difficult to isolate in humans the contributions of the factors of maturation and learning for they continually interact. Clearly however the lungs are well-developed at birth though no air can have entered before birth to distend and exercise them. The complex structures have matured ready to play their part in breathing. Later the child, singer and athlete learn to modify their breathing but these learned modifications are based on the original unlearned act. Similarly the new-born infant can yawn but in the student this act although essentially the same in its motor aspect may become organized as part of his social – and anti-social – behaviour. Innate responses and learned responses thus build up into one system.

The difference between maturation and learning has been clearly demonstrated in birds. Tinbergen[99] showed a model of a bird of prey to very young goslings but they did not respond. At a later age however they did respond by taking avoiding action even though they had during the growing-up period never seen a bird of prey and had been isolated from their mother so that they could not learn from her. Tinbergen[100] reports that 'Grohmann prevented young pigeons from carrying out their incipient flight movements . . . by rearing them in narrow tubes, thus mechanically preventing them from moving their wings. When the controls were able to fly a certain distance, both experimental and control birds were submitted to a simple flying test and it was found that the achievements of the two groups were equal'. It can be concluded from this that flying is not learned, for the experimental pigeons had had no practice, no instruction and no chance to see others fly.

People often talk about children 'learning' to walk but here again maturation plays by far the greatest if not the whole part. It has been reported by Bühler[101] that Albanian children were bound fast in swaddling clothes in their cradles so that they could not move hand or foot. When at first unbound at one year of age they were unable to hold anything, but, within two hours, they could perform tests appropriate to their age. After a short practice period they sat upright, crawled and walked. Other studies have supported this observation that walking is chiefly the result of maturation though it is obviously capable of modification. The race-walking expert for instance has modified and developed further this genetically determined act.

When the organs or systems have matured so that they are ready for use, then using them will help to develop and maintain good functional condition. In the case of the Albanian children lack of practice had not checked maturation but, although these children could within a very short time perform those acts which other children had been practising for months, they nevertheless carried out the movements with more clumsiness than normal children. If a child has matured so that he is ready for a particular activity but the environment does not necessitate the trying out of that activity then it may not occur. At a later date because of what has gone on in the interval it may prove difficult to do. For example the adult may not learn to skate or ride as easily as the youngster. Maturation and development through activity are thus closely interlinked, and it is easy to attribute to training an improvement in performance which is really the result of maturation. An awareness of the contributions of both maturation and development through activity is valuable, particularly as the latter is closely associated with the environment and can therefore be controlled to a large extent (see Plate 1).

Therefore if it is desired that a child at a later age should have a great variety of actions at his command he must be provided with opportunities and ideas at the time when he has matured sufficiently to try them out. If the child tries before he is ready he may get frustrated to the point of impeding his progress later on and he will certainly be wasting his time. McGraw[102] observed that when Johnny did finally learn to ride a tricycle he seemed to suffer somewhat from the long and futile practice undertaken earlier.

Hilgard[103] investigated learning and maturation in children aged 24 to 36 months. The practice group of 10 children was given 12 weeks of practice, with instruction and encouragement, in climbing on and off a table. They were timed at 2-week intervals on climbing up a three-step ladder $2\frac{1}{2}$ feet high, stepping on a table and then climbing down again. The control group was tested at the end of 12 weeks, given 4 days of practice and re-tested. At the end of 12 weeks the performance of the practice group was markedly better than the control but after the 4-days' practice, scores of both groups were similar. Dusenberry[104] found evidence which suggested that, as a result of specific training in ball-throwing, 3- and 4-year-olds showed very little improvement which could possibly be related to that training whereas 5- and 6-year-olds did show marked improvement. Time spent on practice can then be wasteful if carried out at the wrong age.

It has been argued from time to time that intensive practice before maturity of any capacity might stimulate and increase the rate of growth of that capacity but there is no evidence to support this view. On the contrary Gates and Taylor[105] showed that this was not so in the case of speed of tapping by 4- to 6-year-old children and they interpreted their results to mean that long continued training, motivated as effectively as practicable, did not improve the neural and other machinery either directly or indirectly.

It would then be advantageous to know when a person has matured to a point where he should try certain activities since practice before this point is largely a waste of time and may even be harmful because of the frustration and dislike it may cause. On the other hand if left until long after that time then a person may find it very much more difficult to learn the activity. In other words there are 'critical' periods and knowledge of when these are is vitally important if it is desired that some particular skill shall be acquired. In educational gymnastics however where skill in specific activities is not a major aim, every child in a class can be helped to find his own 'critical' periods for particular movements and actions. A disadvantage of set pieces of work in the gymnasium is that, in any school class based on age and academic standard, the physiological age range is likely to be considerable and so only some of the children will be learning the activity at the best possible time for them.

The level of initial ability from which a child starts to learn a new skill contains a large maturational element but it also depends on the previous activity of the structures. Clearly the greater a person's chronological age the more time he will have had to try out and develop different movements and acts but the extent to which he has built up a variety of responses will to a large extent have depended on his environment. A girl who has grown up with two brothers, one older and one younger than herself, is likely to be able to throw a ball better than another girl of the same physiological and chronological age who is an only child. Because she has a well-developed overarm throw she may then learn a good tennis service with less practice than another girl who has mostly thrown underarm. Again boys who go to a school where good systematic instruction is given in cricket are likely to have acquired more skill than those who go to a school where the game is played under the eye of masters whose job is merely to see that they do not get up to any mischief.

The best age at which to try particular activities will then depend not only on the stage of maturation or the physiological age of the child but also on chronological age and on the activities in which he has engaged since birth. Few studies have been made and so most decisions concerning the best age are based on known physiological facts and on the experience of teachers.

The kinds of facts which must be taken into account include such things as the change with age in the size, shape and tissue composition, reaction time, speed, precision, steadiness and strength of every child. It is apparent for instance that size, shape and tissue composition affect the position of the centre of gravity and therefore balance. Not until a child reaches puberty do his proportions begin to approximate those of an adult. A new-born baby with his relatively large head and poorly developed legs has a centre of gravity when in an erect position near the level of the xiphoid (the lower part of the breastbone). As the child gets older and his proportions gradually change so does his centre of gravity gradually move lower down the body. At five to six years it is just below the level of the umbilicus and and at about thirteen years it is below the level of the crest of the ilium (hipbone). Therefore the younger child will find balance in an erect position more difficult than the older and this may affect the ease with which he learns certain skills. On the other hand balance upside down may present more of a problem to the older child though of course there are other factors such as steadiness and muscular control to be taken into account. Tissue composition also affects a body in water. A certain number of boys are 'sinkers' so that, when perfectly still in water, their whole body is below the surface. Kinnear[106] found that out of 250 boys aged eleven to eighteen, 15 per cent were non-floaters. It is obviously easier for a 'floater' to learn to swim and it therefore seems likely that a good time for boys to tackle the activity would be when they had their highest proportion of fat. This is between the ages of ten to fourteen or before pubescence.

Then again, compared with an adult's bones, the bones of a child contain a proportionately greater part of water and soft protein-like materials and a considerably lesser proportion of mineral substances. The skeletal constituents also contain more cartilagenous and fibrous tissue. The bones of a child are therefore more pliable and elastic than those of an adult. At the same time the child's capacity for speed is limited and his weight is comparatively small so his momentum in motion is relatively low. These two facts of a pliable skeleton and low momentum mean that the young child is less likely than the adult to suffer bone fractures or other injury when he collides with some object or when he falls. This is one reason why childhood is a good time in which to learn to skate or ride or ski. At the same time the pliable skeleton means that there is less resistance to stresses and strains than there is in the adult and so tasks

75

involving sustained effort especially if they involve an awkward posture should not be demanded.

Increases in strength appear to go hand in hand with the process of maturation (see Table 4) and in boys there is a marked spurt[107] in strength at adolescence. Thus skills requiring a large minimal strength for their performance might well be left until late adolescence so far as boys are concerned. With regard to endurance events Astrand[108] has said that 'as the aerobic capacity is relatively as great for younger children as for male adults, the children should also be capable of doing prolonged, strenuous exercise'. But capability does not necessarily mean that endurance events are desirable. Astrand goes on to point out that in order to engage in such events careful and regular training over a long period of time is necessary and that 'such a training plan is impossible for children to undergo, it does not fit their mentality. Thus the motive for the choice of events in school and junior sports is first of all a psychological and pedagogical one, not a physiological and medical'. It is generally agreed that short and sharp periods of varied physical activities should be

TABLE 4

GRIPPING STRENGTH (RIGHT-HAND)

| Age | Boys | | | Girls | | | Percentage of terminal score | |
|---|---|---|---|---|---|---|---|---|
| | | | | | | | Boys' | Girls' |
| | N | Mean (kg) | S.D. | N. | Mean (kg) | S. D. | grip strength | grip strength |
| 11 | 65 | 25·14 | 4·09 | 66 | 21·04 | 3·86 | 44·7 | 58·8 |
| 11·5 | 87 | 26·28 | 3·89 | 89 | 22·62 | 4·82 | 46·7 | 63·2 |
| 12 | 93 | 27·62 | 3·71 | 92 | 24·15 | 4·89 | 49·1 | 67·5 |
| 12·5 | 90 | 29·37 | 4·42 | 88 | 26·36 | 5·03 | 52·2 | 73·7 |
| 13 | 92 | 30·96 | 4·60 | 92 | 27·72 | 5·20 | 55·0 | 77·5 |
| 13·5 | 92 | 33·39 | 5·68 | 80 | 28·72 | 4·97 | 59·3 | 80·2 |
| 14 | 89 | 36·33 | 6·96 | 79 | 29·19 | 5·21 | 64·6 | 81·6 |
| 14·5 | 84 | 39·55 | 7·24 | 79 | 30·34 | 5·60 | 70·3 | 84·8 |
| 15 | 84 | 43·40 | 7·15 | 76 | 32·50 | 5·32 | 77·1 | 90·8 |
| 15·5 | 77 | 46·62 | 7·35 | 77 | 33·08 | 5·62 | 82·9 | 92·4 |
| 16 | 76 | 49·10 | 7·09 | 72 | 33·69 | 5·59 | 87·3 | 94·1 |
| 16·5 | 77 | 51·74 | 6·82 | 75 | 34·61 | 5·19 | 92·0 | 96·7 |
| 17 | 77 | 54·50 | 7·06 | 71 | 35·15 | 5·47 | 97·0 | 98·2 |
| 17·5 | 62 | 56·26 | 7·25 | 58 | 35·79 | 5·05 | 100 | 100 |

From *Motor Performance and Growth*, by H. E. Jones, page 37. University of California Press, Berkeley and Los Angeles, 1949.

engaged in with children and that therefore certain activities are inappropriate before adolescence.

Motor co-ordination also improves from birth but when measured by the Brace[109] test little change in girls seems to occur after about thirteen years of age. Boys on the other hand continue to improve and there even appears to be a spurt in late adolescence. There is a popular belief that adolescents are awkward and clumsy and many teachers think that there is a loss in skill when the adolescent spurt in height and weight takes place. They argue that the sudden, uneven and relatively large increases in size must upset co-ordination and balance because the adolescent now has to manipulate levers of a different length and weight and, in the case of boys, has to deal with a sudden increase in strength as well. There is however no proof of a loss in motor co-ordination at puberty. The evidence shows a consistent improvement with chronological age though the *rate of gain* may be retarded in some elements. Dimock[110] and Espenschade[111] have both produced evidence which shows that improvement in motor co-ordination continues even during the periods of the most rapid increases in height and weight. However the amount of improvement in co-ordination is often less at puberty. For example Espenschade, Dable and Schoendube[112] showed that the *rate of gain* in balance is retarded with boys between the ages of thirteen and fifteen. But, as Tanner[113] has said, 'according to the longitudinal data a clumsy boy in late adolescence is likely to have been a clumsy child before adolescence'.

Reaction time, speed, precision and steadiness also all improve as the child matures and therefore if a performance depends primarily on any of these factors early practice has limited and often doubtful value. Certainly the time could be spent to more advantage on some other skill.

Many investigators since Bliss[114] have collected data on motor performance which can be used as a guide when deciding on the ages at which to introduce particular activities. Examples of such data are given in Tables 5, 6 and 7. Another example of this type of work is by Kulcinski.[115] He states that the back somersault, back handspring, handwalk, handstand, front somersault and elbow lever are too difficult for eleven and twelve-year-olds in the sense that, although a few might be

## TABLE 5

MEANS AND STANDARD DEVIATIONS OF PHYSICAL GROWTH AND MOTOR PERFORMANCE OF FIRST, SECOND AND THIRD-GRADE BOYS AND GIRLS (AGE RANGE 6 YEARS 11 MONTHS TO 8 YEARS 11 MONTHS).

| | Grade I | | | | Grade II | | | | Grade III | | | |
|---|---|---|---|---|---|---|---|---|---|---|---|---|
| | Mean | | S.D. | | Mean | | S.D. | | Mean | | S.D. | |
| | Boys | Girls | Boys | Girls | Boys | Girls | Boys | Girls | Boys | Girls | Boys | Girls |
| Number in sample | 89 | 67 | | | 93 | 89 | | | 90 | 82 | | |
| Age | 78·93 | 78·35 | 4·98 | 4·74 | 91·03 | 89·88 | 6·71 | 5·14 | 103·40 | 101·57 | 7·16 | 5·60 |
| Height | 47·75 | 46·95 | 2·30 | 1·79 | 50·90 | 49·80 | 2·16 | 2·46 | 53·38 | 52·10 | 2·34 | 2·42 |
| Weight | 51·82 | 49·19 | 6·50 | 7·90 | 58·94 | 58·32 | 6·92 | 12·87 | 67·43 | 61·67 | 10·95 | 9·28 |
| Dash | 9·30 | 9·51 | 1·20 | 1·12 | 8·28 | 9·00 | ·66 | ·89 | 7·97 | 8·64 | ·60 | ·69 |
| Stick Test (Balance Test) | 5·02 | 5·17 | 4·04 | 5·61 | 7·59 | 5·07 | 6·69 | 5·42 | 9·19 | 10·50 | 8·22 | 9·42 |
| Sidestep (Agility Test) | 9·10 | 8·90 | 1·50 | 1·44 | 9·60 | 9·79 | 1·31 | 2·66 | 11·00 | 10·59 | 1·52 | 1·52 |
| Jump | 34·97 | 35·62 | 6·60 | 5·45 | 38·45 | 35·22 | 5·92 | 6·51 | 44·00 | 41·96 | 6·12 | 6·93 |
| Ball Throw | 137·86 | 71·66 | 50·40 | 27·09 | 176·04 | 82·14 | 51·94 | 30·78 | 216·06 | 108·01 | 57·34 | 33·68 |
| Striking | 4·70 | 4·33 | 2·60 | 1·84 | 5·40 | 4·46 | 2·24 | 1·69 | 5·60 | 5·33 | 2·01 | 1·73 |
| Catching | 6·60 | 6·43 | 2·50 | 2·48 | 8·40 | 7·61 | 1·70 | 2·08 | 9·00 | 9·81 | 1·50 | 1·58 |

*From* 'The relationship between measure of physical growth and gross motor performance of primary grade schoolchildren' *by L. G. Seils. Res. Qtly.* Vol. 22, 1951, pp. 244–60.

*Age*

## TABLE 6

MEANS AND STANDARD DEVIATIONS OF PERFORMANCE SCORES OF GIRLS
AT AGES 6 to 14 YEARS.

| | Run – 30 yds. (Running Start) Seconds | | | Jump (in inches) | | |
|---|---|---|---|---|---|---|
| Age | No. | Mean | S.D. | No. | Mean | S.D. |
| 6 | 26 | 6·37 | ·70 | 26 | 40·5 | 7·1 |
| 7 | 49 | 5·85 | ·58 | 59 | 43·5 | 6·6 |
| 8 | 54 | 5·56 | ·50 | 67 | 47·7 | 5·8 |
| 9 | 64 | 5·24 | ·41 | 81 | 52·9 | 7·6 |
| 10 | 80 | 5·02 | ·44 | 77 | 57·6 | 7·4 |
| 11 | 73 | 4·79 | ·61 | 73 | 61·5 | 7·4 |
| 12 | 42 | 4·60 | ·42 | 47 | 63·9 | 6·0 |
| 13 | 24 | 4·42 | ·48 | 22 | 68·0 | 6·2 |
| 14 | 12 | 4·25 | ·50 | 12 | 69·7 | 6·2 |

From 'Motor Performance of Girls age 6 to 14 years', by R. B. Glassow, and P. Kruse. *R. Q*, Vol. 31, No. 3, 1960, pp. 426–33.

able to learn them, the time and effort necessary is too great in proportion to the number of children of this age who can acquire them. Much of this work has been done on American children and standards for English children may be different.

Apart from physiological factors the interests of the children must also be taken into account for, as will be seen later, motivation is of major importance in learning. It is not easy to describe the physical interests of children of varying ages because it depends not only on maturational age but also to a very large extent on accepted social behaviour – and, of course, there will always be wide individual differences. Nevertheless certain tendencies of particular age groups may be discerned.

The pre-school child usually prefers to be on his own or with one other child and to engage in exploratory and imaginative play oblivious of others. In the first years at school the child willingly takes part in games of the undefined group type in which any number of children take part. For instance in follow-my-leader the children enjoy copying the leader or each other. The child's interest however is in his own actions and not in those of other children nor of the group as a whole. At this time he begins to try out all kinds of movements like jumping,

79

TABLE 7

| Activity and measures used in scoring | Age | Boys Means | S.D. | Girls Means | S.D. |
|---|---|---|---|---|---|
| 35-yds. dash – timed | | | | | |
| in secs. (1) | 5 | 9·30 | | 9·70 | |
| | 6 | 8·52 | | 8·84 | |
| | 7 | 7·92 | | 8·02 | |
| 50-yds. dash– timed | | | | | |
| in secs. (2) | 13·25 | 7·53 | ·50 | 7·84 | ·56 |
| (Longitudinal study | 14·25 | 7·22 | ·53 | 7·88 | ·53 |
| on 80 girls and 85 | 15·25 | 7·08 | ·54 | 7·99 | ·45 |
| boys) | | | | | |
| Soccer kick – distance | 5 | 11·5 | | 8·00 | |
| in ft. (1) | 6 | 18·4 | | 10·10 | |
| | 7 | 25·4 | | 15·00 | |
| Standing broad jump – | | | | | |
| in in. (3) | 7 | 41·6 | | 39·9 | *Note* a |
| (Best of 12 trials) | | | | | |
| (Children had had | 9 | 49·8 | | 47·7 | *Note* b |
| no previous train- | | | | | |
| ing in the jump) | 11 | 59·8 | | 53·8 | *Note* c |
| Standing broad jump – | | | | | |
| in in. (2) | 13·25 | 72·1 | 5·67 | 67·8 | 6·31 |
| | 14·25 | 76·8 | 6·75 | 66·1 | 6·76 |
| | 15·25 | 84·6 | 9·37 | 64·3 | 7·94 |
| | 16·25 | 88·6 | 10·16 | 63·1 | 7·88 |
| Distance throw (base- | | | | | *Note* d |
| ball) in ft. (2) | 13·25 | 116·1 | 19·12 | 70·7 | 15·76 |
| | 14·25 | 123·4 | 29·94 | 74·7 | 17·28 |
| | 15·25 | 131·4 | 24·64 | 74·3 | 18·16 |
| | 16·25 | 144·8 | 17·87 | 72·9 | 18·97 |

Notes *a* Difference not significant (t = 1·8) *b;* Difference significant at 5 per cent level (t = 2·2) *c;* Difference significant at 1 per cent level (t = 5.0) *d;* Difference between means significant in each case.

(1) *Educational Psychology* – Gates, A. I., Jersild, A. T., McConnell T. R., & Challman A. C., Macmillan and Co., New York, 1949, p. 65 as adapted from Jenkins – 'A comparative study of motor achievement of children'.

(2) Espenschade, A. 'Motor Performance in Adolescence.' *Monographs of the Society for Research in Child Development.* Vol. V, No. 1, 1940.

(3) Kane, R. J. and Meredith, H. V. (1952). 'Ability in the standing broad jump of elementary schoolchildren 7, 9 and 11 years of age.' *R. Q.*, 23, p. 198–208.

climbing, turning somersaults, standing on his head, skipping, cycling and bouncing balls. 'Look at me' is a popular request.

From about the age of seven to eleven is the great age for the development of personal motor co-ordinations of all kinds. Up to about the age of nine the child's main source of enjoyment is in the free expression of movement. He simply likes to be energetic and to try out new actions and he will often make superfluous movements for sheer joy. In the ninth or tenth year he begins to take an interest in making his actions effective and efficient and to try to achieve particular levels of performance. He begins to want to do well in sports and games and to become skilled in them. He still, however, finds it difficult to sustain attention even for the length of time of a game of hockey or football or cricket. The time-dimension of a child grows with age but he cannot be expected before the age of about eleven to grasp long-term objectives and so, as already pointed out in the case of endurance, he cannot appreciate the value of training or of practice unless it is for an objective which can be realized almost immediately. Even if he is specially interested in a particular activity he is unlikely to want to spend long periods at it. Alternatively he may be very keen and work very hard at something for several days or even weeks and then suddenly drop it altogether. Minor games, chasing and fighting, are particularly popular with both sexes at this time.

At about eleven years of age competition and team games become important. At first the child merely wants to show that he is better than the other children and even in a team game will probably treat all the other players as opponents. He may also go through a stage when he wants the other players on his side to do what he tells them to do. Gradually, however, he learns that he cannot dominate the group and that he must co-operate with them and limit the part which he plays in his team. Anyone who has tried to teach eleven-year-olds netball or association football will know how difficult it is to stop all the children chasing the ball all the time. This is not due to selfishness or lack of intelligence but to lack of maturity. The age has not been reached where the idea of team co-operation can be grasped. Later most of the children become good team players.

Later still the boy or girl tends to concentrate on those sports in which he or she excels though, given an encouraging environment, many adolescents with only average ability will continue to play and enjoy team games. Nevertheless many boys and even more girls begin to lose interest in them by the time they are fifteen and many lose interest altogether in physical recreation. Given the opportunity, however, adolescents will take part enthusiastically in physical activities such as dancing, lawn tennis, badminton, table tennis and cycling which have a social side where they can meet the opposite sex or in individual skills such as golf, ski-ing, sailing, climbing, motor-cycle scrambling and pot-holing. Activities which offer a tough physical challenge appeal particularly to the young men.

The child then is not a miniature adult. He has different proportions, different physical and mental attributes, different interests and desires. He is indeed a different being and so what are good methods of skill acquisition for the older person must be appropriately varied for the child. It is useless and possibly harmful to try to get a child to acquire a skill before he has matured sufficiently. But even when an individual is ready from the maturational point of view to try an activity the question of how this should be done arises. Should the opportunity to learn on his own be provided or should specific training be given? It has sometimes been assumed that if opportunities are present, children will avail themselves of them. In the most elementary functions this is probably true but as the skills become more complex so does specific training become more vital. Mirenva[116] trained the less able member of four pairs of identical twins aged 4 to $4\frac{1}{2}$ years in jumping and in throwing and rolling balls at targets. After $4\frac{1}{2}$ months of exercises which included the above activities the twins were compared. In every case the trained twin equalled or did better than the twin who had had no specific training but who had, of course, engaged in general activity. Mirenva, however, found that the rate of development was different according to the type of activity and he concluded from his results that an elementary motor function or basic movement such as jumping in the air develops very rapidly whether a person is trained or not, whereas training plays a very much greater role in the development of the more complex skills such as hitting targets with balls.

It seems probable then that those basic movements such as elementary running, climbing and jumping in which the maturational factor plays a great part should be allowed to develop by provision of opportunity, example, ideas, encouragement and general practice. The chance of seeing many different things, of exploring many different environments and of trying out many diverse movements should be given to every child. When, however, the child begins to want to jump over something, throw at a target of some kind, perform recognized gymnastic vaults, skate, ride, run races, swim, dive and so on, then specific training is beneficial and the general rules given in the previous chapter, apply. The training must be at the right mental and physical level for the particular child – too much concentration, depths of understanding, strength or time should not be required.

In general the period from five to the beginning of adolescence should be one in which a great variety of personal skills and techniques are not only encouraged but also taught. Team games come into their own in early adolescence and later, more selection and specialization takes place. This matter of specialization must be considered. If it is desired that a person should be as skilled as possible in one particular activity by the time he is an adult, then it may be that he should spend all the time he has for physical activity on training in that skill. This seems to be the modern tendency and cases can be cited of children who have spent a great deal of time from early childhood on a major game or sport and have become outstanding in that activity. There have also been many child prodigies who have failed as adults and in this case they have probably missed a great deal through not acquiring other skills. There have also been others who have given up the activity as soon as they have felt themselves able to do so. Some of these have been children who were not driven by a basic interest and pleasure in the activity but by other incentives such as wishing to please their parents. Later this does not suffice and the very fact that the child has spent much time on practising one activity when this was not a natural thing to do, may have destroyed any interest which might have been there had the skill been allowed to develop more slowly. Certainly no one can acquire outstanding skill in any complex activity unless he is highly motivated and external pressures may adversely affect motivation, temporarily or permanently.

Decisions on the best time to specialize must depend to a large extent on the ultimate aims of any individual. If maximum proficiency in a particular skill is a major objective then it may be that this will only be attained if the skill is practised as soon as the child is mature enough to try it at all. Obviously there are great risks in this so far as the development of the child as a whole is concerned and the resultant deficiencies must be taken into account. But in any case evidence is scanty and it could equally well be argued that a child who acquires a wide range of skills before puberty may in the long run also make a better specialist. As a child grows he continually has to adjust his skill to his changing abilities and proportions and therefore a great deal of time spent in the early years on a major sport or game may well be spent uneconomically in the sense that it could have resulted in greater improvement and enjoyment elsewhere.

So far changes only until adulthood have been considered. But when a person becomes an adult he does not attain a fixed state. He continues to change though for many years the changes are not so apparent as in childhood. It has been shown for instance that height begins to decline once adult stature is attained[117] and it is interesting to look at the curves of growth and decline shown in Figs. 9 and 10. These were based on data collected in Francis Galton's[118] first anthropometric laboratory at the Health Exhibition at South Kensington in 1884.

Welford [119] has stated that 'as regards bodily mechanism the progress from young adulthood onwards is essentially one of gradual deterioration'. This physical deterioration which may occur 'in the central control and guidance of actions' as well as in the sensory and effector organs is not necessarily reflected in performance because an older person, if he wishes to do so, is able in a very large number of activities to compensate for physical deficiencies by a wiser use of his abilities. The opportunity to compensate will be determined by the relative importance in the activity of the anatomical and physiological machinery. Thus one might expect that top-class sprinters will be young because here the bodily mechanism is all-important. In hurdling, high-jumping and even more in the pole-vault an older man may be able to maintain his place by attaining a very high level of skill in the muscular co-ordinations required

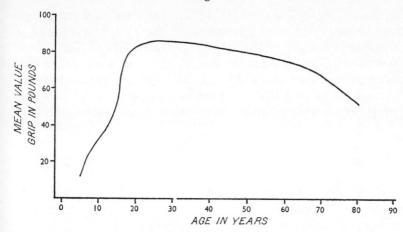

Fig. 9. Age and grip of stronger hand, means males. From H. A. Ruger and B. Stoessiger, 1927.

for the particular event. Where care, accuracy, tactical know-ledge and 'cunning' can improve performance, as for example in golf and lawn tennis, the older man can continue at a very high standard and often more than hold his own for quite a long time. This can be seen from Tables 8 and 9 and Fig. 11. Jokl[120] has reported that women of 45 and men of 66 took part

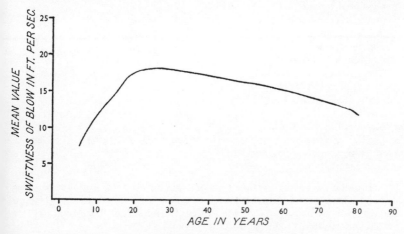

Fig. 10. Age and swiftness of blow, means males. From H. A. Ruger and B. Stoessiger, 1927.

in the Olympic Games in Helsinki in 1952 and that the results of a competition arranged specially for elderly gymnasts in Germany showed very little deterioration with age. The trained 60-year-olds had a running speed which was higher than that of untrained men of 40. The performance of women between the ages of 32 and 45 in a 75-metre dash, shot-putt and broad jump did not change at all. Normally of course performances of

TABLE 8
PARTICIPANTS IN THE OLYMPIC GAMES IN HELSINKI 1952
Age Range in Years

|  | Women | Men |
|---|---|---|
| Swimming | 14–36 | 13–45 |
| Canoeing | 20–38 | 20–36 |
| Fencing | 16–45 | 20–49 |
| Apparatus Gymnastics | 16–36 | 15–45 |
| Track and field events | 18–38 | 15–42 |

From 'Age and Physical Activity', by E. Jokl., *Coaching Newsletter*, July, 1957.

TABLE 9
SUMMARY OF FINDINGS WITH REFERENCE TO PROFICIENCY AT SPORTS AND GAMES

| Types of Activity | Number of cases[1] | Mean Age | Standard Deviation | Years of maximum proficiency |
|---|---|---|---|---|
| Professional boxers (world champions) | 448 | 26·98 | 3·98 | 25–26 |
| Bantamweights |  | 24·83 |  |  |
| Heavyweights |  | 29·79 |  |  |
| Professional ice-hockey (N. American Continent) | 823 | 27·56 | 4·00 | 24–25 |
| Amateur tennis players (national championships England, France and U.S. ) | 317 | 27·63 | 5·25 | 25–27 |
| Professional baseball (excluding pitchers) | 3126 | 29·07 | 4·04 | 28 |
| Golf (Open championships England and U.S.) | 88 | 31·01 | 6·37 | 25–34 |

[1] Number of cases does not mean the number of individuals. For example there were 133 world champions concerned in the boxing figures and perhaps 500 to 600 different individual base-ball players which contributed to the 3,126 player–years.
From 'The most proficient years at sports and games', by H. C. Lehman. *R.Q.* Vol. 9, 1938, pp. 3–19.

older people in many physical activities deteriorate because of lack of interest and motivation.

It has been shown that age has an effect on initial ability and that where there is neuromuscular immaturity or lack of strength or some other necessary prerequisite, learning will be slow. It may now be asked whether age affects the rate of learning when the necessary abilities are present. The answer to this question is by no means clear because of the difficulty of

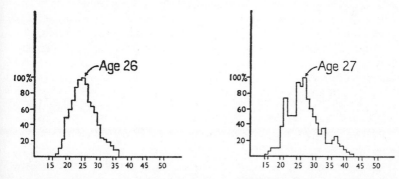

Fig. 11. *Left:* Chronological ages at which 133 boxers won or retained 448 world championship titles—all weight classifications. *Right:* Chronological ages at which 317 national tennis championships (English, American, and French) were either first won or retained. From H. C. Lehman, 1938.

N.B. Peak of each distribution was arbitrarily assigned a value of 100% and the rest were assigned proportionate percentage values.

measuring the practice effect alone. Munn[121] states that 'beyond the early years of childhood, when the handicaps of neuromuscular immaturity have largely been overcome, practically all differences in the learning of children and adults may be attributed to differences in motivation and in previous experience. Our discussion of motor skills, for example, demonstrated that, although older children and adults may begin with higher scores than younger children, the percentage of improvement resulting from a given amount of practice is alike regardless of age'. Data from an experiment by Henry and Nelson[122] seem to substantiate this viewpoint. Can then a much older person learn as fast as a youngster? One can find cases of sportsmen who have learned golf at a relatively late age at an apparently fast rate and old men can acquire a very high degree of skill at bowls but these may be due to high initial ability. Welford [123] and his co-workers have conducted several experiments into this question.

In one experiment made up of three parts the subjects each time threw 50 loops of light chain 3 inches in length at a target made up of 49 three-inch square open-topped boxes which slanted forward at an angle of about 45°. Each subject was given the task under three conditions. In one the subject threw directly at the target over a distance of 8 feet. In the second the conditions were the same except that he had to throw over a horizontal bar set 32 inches from the ground 5 feet away. In the third the subject had to throw over a screen of the same height in place of the bar. The screen hid the target from direct view but it could be seen in a mirror placed behind it. The target was turned round so that the subject could obtain knowledge of his results by looking in the mirror. To balance practice effects the three conditions were presented in different orders to different subjects within each age-range. The 84 subjects who took part were divided into age-ranges as follows: 12 from fifteen to nineteen, 12 in the twenties, 24 in the thirties, 18 in the forties and 18 in the fifties.

In direct throwing and in throwing over the bar there was no evidence of any deterioration of performance as regards either accuracy or time taken. In throwing over the screen, however, there was a pronounced rise in the far-near inaccuracy from the thirties to the fifties. What is more interesting is that there was a rise with age of the differences between inaccuracy in this condition and in throwing over the bar and also a rise in the differences in time taken between throwing over the bar and over the screen. The increased difficulty could not have been due to failing vision nor to failure of the effector mechanisms – since no falling off in performance for these reasons was shown in the other conditions – but must have been the result of the complication of the perceptual task. It is apparent therefore that the locus of the increased difficulty shown by the older subjects must have lain within the central mechanisms of the receptor side.

As a result of this and other experiments Welford states that 'it would appear that, as a person gets older, he finds it increasingly difficult to *comprehend* verbal or visual data, especially when these are in any way new or unfamiliar'. To put it another way the older person is able to deal fairly well with a situation which can be adequately met by means of what he brings to it from the past but finds it difficult to learn a task which is new in some important way. It is not clear to what extent the difficulty arises from deterioration in the central mechanisms or is due to previous experience impeding the fresh organization of in-coming data or outgoing action. It may well be that this again is a case of age affecting initial ability – in this case dis-advantageously – rather than age affecting the rate of learning.

Perhaps this question of the effect of age on rate of learning alone is rather academic and need not concern us too much since it is the total result which is of chief interest. It may then be concluded that the effect of age on rate of learning is not clear but that the speed with which a given level of performance is reached is related to chronological age and even more to physiological age. In general, motor performance improves with age up to maturity. There is then a longish period during which there may be a gradual decline or, where care and accuracy or experience are important ingredients of success, progress may continue. Welford 'found evidence that older people can maintain an established skill to an age considerably beyond that at which they can without undue difficulty learn a new skill'. Ultimately, however, performance begins to deterior-ate. Though this deterioration can be due to changes in the sensory organs and in the cardio-vascular, respiratory and muscular systems, it can also arise because of the slowing down of the discrimination and choice processes in the central ner-vous system. Crossman and Szafran[124] have produced evidence that in some tasks 'the limiting factors lie rather in the central non-specific part of the total mechanism than in either the peripheral sensory or motor systems'.

## (2) SEX

A large number of experimental comparisons have been made in the rate of learning of various skills by males and females. For example Kulcinski[125] found the eleven- and twelve-year-old girls in his experimental group superior on average to the boys in the learning of agilities such as cartwheels, handspring, elbow stand and forearm stand. On the other hand he found more boys than girls able to do the long dive, neck dive and squat stand after training. This result was quite typical for differences have been found sometimes in favour of one sex and sometimes the other but no consistent difference in learning ability has been shown to exist. Given individuals of both sexes who are of equal initial ability and equally motivated, it appears that the same amount of practice will produce the same amount of improvement. But differences in rate of learning do arise even in boys and girls with equal initial ability because of differences in interest. It is important however to realize that these differences in interest are largely determined by social factors rather than by any innate differences due to sex. Margaret Mead[126] has shown that 'the personalities of the two sexes are socially produced'. In one primitive society there was 'a genuine reversal of the sex-attitudes of our own culture, with the women the dominant, impersonal, managing partner, the man the less responsible and the emotionally dependent person'. Although basic physical structures and attributes may affect interests their contribution is uncertain and what evidence there is shows that most differences result from social tradition and social pressures.

Allowing for this, however, it is of value to know the differences which may be expected to arise in our own society. These differences affect not only interest but also, after the first few years of life, initial ability for any particular skill. If skipping is considered to be a feminine act and throwing stones a suitable activity for boys, the majority of boys and girls will later differ in their initial abilities for other activities. The average American schoolboy does better than the average American schoolgirl in most tests of strength and speed and in many motor skills. This is illustrated in Tables 4, 5 and 7.

It should perhaps be pointed out that these results refer to American schoolchildren and that only one test of balance, in which there is some evidence that girls do as well and sometimes better than boys, is included.

There are two matters of importance which should be noted. First that the differences are not very great with young children, that they gradually increase and, although varying from skill to skill, are marked in adolescence. Secondly that any boy may differ more from another boy than he does from some other girl. In other words there is a very considerable overlap which in the early years is so great that separation of the sexes for skill learning is neither desirable nor necessary. The interests and activities of boys and girls are probably more similar between the ages of ten and twelve than at any other time in their development. Even at fourteen years it can be seen from Table 7 that well over one-sixth of the girls can jump farther than one-sixth of the boys. But fairly late in adolescence boys have a spurt in the development of muscular strength which appears to depend largely on maturational factors. Boys therefore like to demonstrate their strength – it is to them a sign of adulthood – and to take part in games and sports of all kinds where they can use a large amount of physical energy. For girls on the other hand the period between thirteen and sixteen seems a difficult one emotionally and there is a tendency for them to go through a period of diminished efficiency.

Major sex differences in physique also arise at adolescence and in so far as these effect initial ability for any particular activity they influence the speed with which any new skill is acquired. From birth until about eleven years of age, boys are slightly heavier and taller than girls, but between the ages of eleven and fifteen there is little difference and for a time girls may even be taller and heavier than boys. This is due to the fact that the growth spurt occurs earlier on average in girls than in boys. After the age of fifteen boys go ahead again with the result that men are in general larger than women. Men also have broader shoulders, narrower hips, longer legs relative to length of body, longer arms particularly forearms and less fat. Again, however, there is a considerable overlap between the sexes. At adolescence physiological changes also occur and cause sex differences in such things as resting systolic blood pressures, resting heart rate, haemoglobin concentration, vital capacity and so on. Tanner[127] has however pointed out that 'It is necessary to add here the warning that sex differences, even in morphology – and far more so in physiology and psychology – are very poorly documented'. Anyone interested in this subject could not do better than to read his book.

Sex then appears to have no effect on rate of learning but in our society does influence average motor performances and therefore also the time taken to learn any new skill.

## (3) INTELLIGENCE

Intelligence and physical ability both improve as a child gets older. In order to consider if there is any relationship between intelligence and physical ability it is therefore necessary to hold age constant or to rule it out of account so that it will not affect results. When this is done it appears that the correlation between intelligence as measured by the usual type of intelligence test and performance in motor skills is positive but it is usually negligible and is certainly never very high.

Hicks[128] correlated mental age with the scores on a test involving hitting a moving target with a ball, for 59 children aged 3 to 6. When chronological age was partialled out so that it did not influence the result, the correlation was $\cdot05 \pm \cdot09$. Reaney[129] found a correlation of $r = \cdot32$ between play ability as shown in group games and general ability but this result is of doubtful value for the ability measures were largely subjective. Thus play ability depended on the estimates by teachers and games captains of the standard of play in hockey and netball in the case of girls and football, hockey and cricket in the case of the boys, and the general ability assessment was based on teacher's estimates or form positions. Oliver[130] tested some educationally sub-normal boys aged 12–15 years whose intelligence quotients varied between 50 and 80 on the Terman and the Porteus Maze intelligence tests, on an athletic achievement test comprising the 50-yard dash, standing broad jump and throwing the cricket ball, and on a 'tennis' test which consisted of standing in a 6-foot circle and having 30 trials at bouncing a ball on a racket to a height of the subject's head. When age was extracted, the following correlations were obtained:

|  | Athletic Achievement | 'Tennis' test total score | 'Tennis' test percentage gain |
|---|---|---|---|
| Terman | $\cdot15$ | $\cdot07$ | $\cdot15$ |
| Porteus Maze | $\cdot32$ | $\cdot40$ | $\cdot20$ |

Many investigations have been reviewed by Burley and Anderson[131] who themselves found no relationship between intelligence test scores and jump and reach test scores. In general, results show that the correlations vary in size but that the majority are near zero and that very few indeed are above $0\cdot5$.

These results indicate that athletes or swimmers or boxers or football players can range widely in intelligence quotients and that people with high or low intelligence test scores can be equally bad or equally good at physical activities.

So far motor performance has been considered and motor performance is related not only to learning ability but also to the amount of practice a person has engaged in and to his interest and motivation. It may therefore be asked whether an individual with a high intelligence quotient will learn a physical skill more speedily then one with a low intelligence quotient given the same opportunities and the same initial ability. Evidence on the relationship between intelligence test scores and the rate of learning physical skills is not easy to obtain because of the difficulty of ensuring similar initial ability. Johnson[132] for instance reported a correlation of minus ·57 between the intelligence quotient of twenty men and the number of trials they required to walk a tight wire. Since the subjects had absolute zero knowledge of tight-wire walking the results indicated that the men of superior intelligence mastered the intricacies of wire walking more readily than those with a lower intelligence rating. Nevertheless it is difficult to suppose that the men were in fact equal in initial ability.

Davies[133] (see also pages 18–20 of this book) reported that in the uninstructed group of students mental ability had little influence on their achievement in archery. 'The brighter students failed to use their ability to determine ways of improving their score. Instead, like the duller ones of the same group, they hit upon and continued to use a method of shooting that gave some initial success.' But she also reported that in the group receiving systematic instruction the brighter students 'tended to profit more by instruction than did the duller students'. The tendency was slight, however, the correlation between mental test scores and archery achievement being ·41. Kulcinski[134] reported 'a definite and positive relationship' between various degrees of intelligence of eleven- and twelve-year-old boys and girls and the learning of fundamental muscular skills of the tumbling and stunt variety but he does not give details. The study was carried out under regular classroom conditions with normal instructional procedures and intelligence quotients ranged from 41–125. Cox[135] on the other hand reported that general intelligence played no part in determining progress under training.

Children with higher intelligence test scores are likely to understand verbal explanation more easily than those with low intelligence quotients and so it is possible that the relationship found in the above studies arises from the type of instruction used. Certainly instruction should be at a level and of a type suitable for the particular learner and it may be advisable to use visual and other means rather than verbal with children having relatively low intelligence test scores.

This question of the relationship between intelligence test scores and the rate of learning physical skills is confused by the fact that it has now been argued by Woodrow[136] that the ability to learn cannot be identified with the ability known as intelligence. Intelligence test scores do not exclude past learning for the tests assume that the background of the subjects has been comparable. Intelligence can therefore have a high correlation with achievement and yet have little correlation with gain due to practice. Woodrow considers that 'individuals possess no such thing as a unitary general learning ability' and points out that certain motor skills 'show no appreciable correlation with intelligence either before or after practice and yet show marked improvement with practice'.

In general it may be said that the mentally retarded show poorer learning but that this may be due in part to inappropriate methods of instruction or to emotional difficulties. Within the normal range there is a positive relationship between intelligence test scores and the performance of physical skills but its size depends on the type of task. It tends to be low particularly in the case of the simpler skills. As the skills become more complex and require more organization and understanding and particularly when decision-making becomes important, the relationship tends to increase but is, even then, rarely substantial.

## (4) INDIVIDUAL DIFFERENCES

Apart from differences arising through age and sex there is also variability in human traits and abilities among persons of the same age and sex. Wechsler[137] has shown that the range (defined as the interval which includes all but the lowest and uppermost 0·1 per cent of the population) of human capacities when reduced to comparable ratios is always found to be small and that a vast majority of the total range ratios fall below 2·85 : 1. But in absolute terms individual differences have a substantial effect on performance. It can be deduced for instance from Table 7 that towards the extremes of the range one boy aged 13·25 might throw a baseball 173·46 feet whereas another might throw it only 58·74 feet, that another boy might jump 89·11 inches and yet another only 55·09 inches and that a girl of the same age might jump 86·73 inches and another only 48·87 inches. Clearly these performances vary enormously.

It should be realized however that neither the best nor the worst performances in (say) the distance throw and the broad jump will necessarily be produced by the same boys. Espenschade[138] found the correlation between the performances in these two events to vary between r = ·39 and r = ·60 and this is a higher relationship than one usually finds between two different activities. Indeed a person who is good in one physical activity is not necessarily even above average in another and it is not possible to predict that an individual will fail in a new physical activity because he has failed in a previous one.

A. INNATE ABILITIES

Attempts have been made to isolate a general motor factor similar in the physical field to general intelligence in the mental. Espenschade reviewed the literature and concluded that 'the weight of evidence does not support the concept of a general motor ability'. Seashore[139] has demonstrated the essential independence of fine and gross motor abilities. McCloy[140] has enumerated fourteen factors in the area of physical and health education which are statistically independent and uncorrelated with each other and has suggested others. Individuals will vary in these basic capacities and their performances will therefore vary according to the relative importance of these capacities in performing particular activities.

Although it seems clear that there is no general motor factor, some evidence of a moderate inter-correlation between gross motor skills of the athletic type has been produced. Highmore [141] found a general factor when he analysed, by factorial analysis, the results from nine athletic tests applied to 240 war veterans whose average age was thirty. He also quotes work by Vernon and Burt to support the idea that there is a general factor of athletic ability. The tests used by Highmore cover a relatively restricted field of athletic endeavour for they consisted of the 50-yard sprint, ¼-mile run, medicine-ball putt, throwing the cricket ball, soccer-ball punt, standing upward jump and the running broad jump. The results from an intelligence test and the Wing rhythm test were not included because they did not correlate with athletic ability as judged by two physical education experts on a five-point rating scale. It should be particularly noted that the competitive element was omitted and that tests requiring a response to ball play were avoided. There is, of course, no way of determining whether there is or is not a general factor from factorial analysis alone. Highmore's general factor for instance may be a group factor because of the limited size of the battery or it may be a consequence of the particular technique of factorial analysis used.

If one considers athletic activity in the broadest sense so that it includes games and sports and dance, then the relationship between the competence in such activities is so low as to make prediction impossible. It is of course true that some do excel in many branches of physical education but there are also many others who excel in one area only. Some of those who excel in many aspects of physical education may do so, not because of above average innate abilities for all of them but either because they are highly motivated to acquire motor accomplishments or more probably because they have had early success in one area. This success, resulting as it often does in encouragement from family, friends and teacher, leads them to tackle other physical activities with more confidence and interest. Frequently too they put in more practice than the average child. Since interest and practice play a major part in the development of skill, such persons are likely to develop their abilities to the maximum and this results in a higher than average all-round level of attainment. Thus there is a very slight tendency for a person who is outstandingly good in one motor performance to be slightly above rather than below average in another, particularly where a high degree of strength is involved. But this tendency is so small as to be negligible, particularly in complex skills.

Certainly we should in practice get away from the idea that people are either 'naturals' for physical activities of all kinds or they are not. If we adopt this attitude we may even be affecting detrimentally many who could develop into very good performers in certain fields and discourage altogether others who could have reached an enjoyable level of attainment. Physical education embraces such a wide variety of activities that it enables individuals with very different basic abilities to find an activity in which those abilities can be used to the best advantage and so give most satisfaction. When we know more about the contribution of particular basic abilities to performance in specific activities we may be better able to advise than we are at present.

There is also another possible reason for the tendency to produce persons who appear to have innate ability in many fields of physical education. In the normal process of growth there are not only wide variations between children but there is a tendency for the child who is advanced at five years to continue to be an 'early-developer' until adulthood and for another who is retarded to reach maturity much later than the average. Early or late development does not imply any abnormality for both are quite usual among very large numbers of the population. This means that early developers will be farther along the path of maturity and that they will therefore tend to be ahead of other children of the same chronological age in motor co-ordination, reaction time, speed, precision, steadiness, etc. Where size is an aid to performance of a skill they will also have the advantage. In boys too there is at adolescence a spurt in strength and since strength is an important factor in the performance of many skills the late-developers will again be under a handicap. All these points mean that the early maturing boy tends to maintain his superiority until he is about sixteen or seventeen or until, in many cases, the end of his school life. It does not however follow that if both had had the same chances and opportunities that, as adults, the late-developers could not be just as good performers. But do they in practice enjoy the same opportunities and encouragement? Since physical prowess particularly in boys is closely associated with prestige in the adolescent culture the early-developers have the praise of their companions to encourage them. If it is the practice of a school or of the controlling body of a sport to select out children for special team or individual coaching at an early age then the late-developers are doubly handicapped. Of course, if the purpose of selection is to produce the best school team then the procedure is a valid one. It may not be valid in the case of special coaching arranged by controlling bodies of sport, for if age is an important factor when selection is made, then early-developers rather than those with the greatest ultimate potential may be the ones to be selected. If, however, our interest is in giving as many as possible a high degree of skill then we must not get preconceived ideas during his school life of a person's ultimate potential and we must beware of giving the child himself any idea of limits to his physical ability. All must be encouraged and properly coached. In many games it is the practice and interest of the individual which counts most in the long run towards the standard of performance which he will reach. This is particularly so where specific skill and not innate abilities plays a preponderant part.

Individuals vary then in their innate abilities. These affect not only initial ability and ultimate capacity but also rate of learning. The rate of learning too will vary according to the type of activity and the method of its presentation to the learner. For example, Carlson and Carr[142] showed that when series of visual recognition tests of words favouring the use of vision alone, vocality alone, and vision and vocality combined, were given to 202 subjects, a considerable number of subjects were consistently superior in one series as contrasted with another. Kay[143] in an experiment with visual and auditory cues found that there were some extreme people who clearly favoured one sensory modality over another in learning and remembering. Thus individuals differ in their ability to use different sensory cues.

### B. ATTRIBUTES ARISING IN PART FROM TRAINING AND FROM PREVIOUS EXPERIENCE

Apart from differences in innate abilities which affect the individual's 'ceiling' in any activity and also the ease with which he learns a particular skill there are also wide differences at any particular moment between individuals of the same age and sex due to their previous experience and training. Strength, flexibility and endurance change in the normal course of maturation but they also can be changed by special exercise and training. It is not intended to go into the methods for doing so since they have been dealt with very adequately elsewhere, for example by Munrow,[144] Karpovitch,[145] Steinhaus.[146] No attempt should be made to learn any particular skill before the minimal physical requirements are present. For example it is inadvisable to try to teach a horizontal astride vault (long-fly) over a vaulting box unless the learners have sufficient strength and spring in the legs to reach the end of the box and sufficient strength to take their own weight on their arms. Indeed any such attempts may in the long run delay the acquisition of the skill.

In some skilled activities there may be different ways of performing the techniques and yet achieving the same general aim. Thus some of the differences in techniques between men and women at hockey, cricket, tennis and squash rackets may arise through different physical attributes and it cannot automatically be assumed that the men's method is the most appropriate one for all. Nevertheless from time to time some activity or method of performing some skill has been declared dangerous for women but sooner or later women have come along and shown the statement to be wrong in their case. In many activities of course physiological factors make a large contribution to performance and where this is so the person with more strength and endurance is likely though not certain to reach a given level of performance more quickly.

It is important here to distinguish between the changes in the central nervous system which are assumed to occur when skill acquisition takes place and other physiological changes – such as increased strength and endurance – which also may occur under conditions of practice. Both types of change may contribute to the level of performance reached in any particular skill. But when an individual is training he should know the effect of his methods on the internal neural process and on the cardiovascular and muscular systems and not assume that a method beneficial to one necessarily aids the others.

For instance an individual learning to shot-putt may wish to build up his strength and power. In order to do this it is normal practice to 'overload' his muscles and cardiovascular system. But if this is done by shot-putting continuously in a long practice session his skill may break down. If he continues nevertheless, then he may find that on the next occasion his skill in terms of the necessary timed muscular co-ordinations has deteriorated even though his strength and power may have increased. Thus it is probably advisable to train for strength, power and endurance by special methods such as weight training and circuit training extraneous to the specific skill if these factors are of such importance to performance that they must be developed more speedily than would happen in the normal course of acquiring the skill. During this build-up, the skill must also be practised otherwise the feel for the necessary motor co-ordinations may be lost. In the case of some skills which are basic in nature such as running it may be possible to train endurance by repetition of the activity without endangering the skill aspect. In swimming too it has been argued that the type of endurance required is specialized to such an extent that it can only be satisfactorily built up in the water. Nunney,[147] for instance, found that an experimental group which spent 30 minutes per week on circuit training and 50 minutes per week on swimming scored a little less well in the endurance swim than did the control group who had spent 90 minutes on swimming. The difference was not however significant. 'Anita Lonsbrough, world record holder, Olympic gold medallist, and Bill O'Donnell, British record holder, 100 yards and 110 yards . . . do very little land work and have never done weight training.'[148] On the other hand Kinnear[149] has pointed out that most countries now include weight training or pulley-weight exercises for strength and muscular endurance, running for stamina training and free standing exercises for mobility as part of the programme for swimmers. In any case the skilled pattern of movements must be thoroughly laid down in the individual first so that the endurance training does not break it down.

In the case of games different questions arise. In racket games for instance the neural process plays such a big part in performance that perfecting the skill takes a long time and during this time adequate strength, power and endurance will, under normal conditions, be built up in the course of practice and competitive play. Special training for physiological factors

1.   Two little girls at play in the garden of their home.   One, just 6 years old, could stand on her head for more than a minute.   The other child, aged 4½ years, had tried for many hours to copy her sister without success (*see* pp. 72-73).

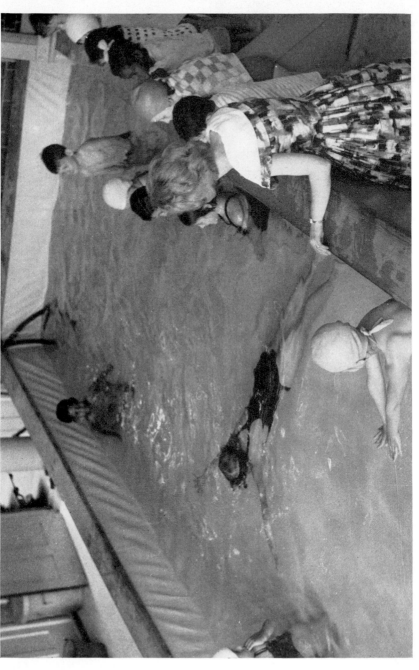

2. A swimming pool constructed in a classroom at Craven Park Primary School, London. As the water level can be adjusted to suit the physical size of the children, whole learning methods can be employed from the

3. The three medallists in the shot-putt at the Olympic Games 1960 show similarity of physique (*see* p. 31). From right to left are Long (bronze), Nieder (gold) and O'Brien (silver).

4. The 100 metres finalists in the Olympic Games 1960 show similarity of physique though there is rather more variation than there is in the case of the shot-putters. From left to right are Hary (1st), Radford (3rd), Figuerola (4th),

5. Tottenham Hotspur's team which achieved the 'double' of F.A. Cup and League Championship show wide variation in physique (*see* pp. 31-32). From left to right, Blanchflower, Brown, Henry, Allen, McKay, Dyson, Baker, Norman, White, Jones, Smith. Blanchflower is fairly light-framed, Dyson is small and wiry, Norman is tall and muscular, Smith is bulky, White is very slim and light-framed and so on.

6. The Italian and British Davis Cup teams show a great variation in physique (*see* p. 31). The players from left to

right are: Moss, Pietrangeli, Merlo, Pickard, Knight and Davies

7. This photograph shows an educational gymnastics group at the University of Birmingham. Educational gymnastics is a whole method of learning and it can be seen that individuals of varying physiques can take part with confidence (*see* p. 65).

8. This photograph shows part learning where the part does not refer to technique but to a division of the whole activity (*see* pp. 67–68). The three players nearest the camera are working as an attacking group towards the cows in ... ... to exploit quickly the numerical superiority of three attackers over two defenders.

are only necessary if the individual has a particular weakness which is holding back his skill performance or if he is unable to get strong enough competition. Even then, unless he has unlimited time at his disposal, he would probably gain more in over-all performance by working on the skill aspects rather than concentrating on the effector mechanisms, for fatigue in racket games is probably as much mental as physical in origin. Sandra Reynolds is reported[150] to have said, after losing to Angela Mortimer at Wimbledon in 1961: 'I knew what I should have done – come to the net more often – but I wasn't allowed to. I wasn't physically tired, it was more mental fatigue.' In many team games the same argument can be applied. Winterbottom[151] has said that conditioning the body to meet the demands of strength, speed and stamina made by the game of association football and to withstand the nervous strain of competition 'should be related as closely as possible to the needs of the activity: ball practice, when it is rightly devised, can do the entire job of getting a player into shape for his game. . . . Clearly the greatest need in any ball game is the perfection of ball-play. A billiards player docs not train by walking round the table; nor will a footballer better his football skill by running around the field. Complete exercise for the body can be provided entirely by footballing activities. The legs can be developed by running with the ball, or jumping to head or catch it; the neck, arms and trunk exercised by throwing-in practices, charging, tackling, goalkeeping and swerving'. At no time however should the skill be continued once there are signs of it breaking down in its effectiveness. For the purpose of building up stamina different skills using the same effector mechanisms can be utilized. If, however, the player begins to lose interest altogether in the skills and the endurance training has not yet been completed, then distance running and exercises could be used. Similarly if the player cannot practise the skills for administrative reasons then mobility, strength and endurance exercises can be valuable provided they are used intelligently and related to the needs of the particular game.

Previous experience also affects initial ability in skill learning and there are therefore wide differences between individuals due to the environment they have encountered since birth. It is now necessary therefore to consider retention and transfer of training.

# VI

## RETENTION, TRANSFER OF TRAINING
## AND MOTIVATION

### (1) RETENTION

IN MOST of the complex skills of physical education perfection is never attained so even the expert may still be considered a learner. Usually therefore he does not practice to keep his skill at a certain level but rather to try to improve it. Outstanding performers are not satisfied to stay with their current form even though it is the best in the world. Nevertheless one may ask how often a skilled person would have to practice to keep his skill 'ticking-over' at its present standard, or to put it another way, how long it would be before the skill is forgotten.

The evidence on this point so far as motor skills are concerned is scanty. In 1906 Swift[152] reported retention of about 63 per cent of his typing speed over a two-year period and later work has borne this out. It does seem that once a person has learned to ride a bicycle or swim that he never quite forgets it. The author succeeded in doing a swimming test involving diving under a boat and swimming 100 yards in very cold water after having done no swimming at all for fourteen years. Johnson[153] reports that men who had learned to walk a tight wire were able to walk it successfully at the first attempt after a lapse of one or two years. It also seems that a highly skilled person can keep up his standard with only occasional practices. On many occasions skilled tennis players after a few hours of practice have performed almost as well as ever after long lay-offs. The author after such a period of no practice actually played better within two months of beginning again than she had ever done before – and this at a mature age.

What factors affect the amount we remember and the amount we forget? In verbal learning pleasant experiences are better retained than unpleasant; material which has been 'overlearned' is better retained than that which has been just learned; and meaningful material is retained more easily than material which has been learned without understanding. In the absence of contrary information it seems probable that the same is true of motor skills. Often verbal material is not remembered exactly but the gist of it is. Similarly in physical skills the basic fundamentals seem to be retained and this may even result on occasions in more effective performance (see p. 51).

It is possible that a small amount of forgetting may occur through lapse of time alone but this is clearly not a major factor. This point needs to be stressed for many young people seem to think that if they have to give up an activity for a time – because of illness or courses of study or domestic duties – that they therefore can never become good at that activity. The effect must depend to a certain extent on the activity for clearly if the best age for peak performance is fifteen then an individual who cannot take part between the ages of fourteen and sixteen is likely to suffer a permanent disadvantage. But this would not be because of deterioration in skill but because of deterioration in innate abilities. In most games, however, maturity of outlook can more than compensate for any fall-off in innate abilities such as speed for some time. A tennis player then who loses three years (say) from seventeen to twenty can still, provided he is strongly motivated, reach his lawn tennis peak. During the three years he is likely to suffer little loss of skill and one has only to look round the tournaments to know that continuous play does not automatically result in continuous improvement. It merely means he will reach his peak at a later age than he might have done.

Of much more significance are the activities which are pursued during the interval. People can go from one winter to another and find that their skill in skating or ski-ing has deteriorated very little. This is because they do not do any similar activities in the interval which may interfere. Whereas the tennis player may find that a season of badminton has interfered with his tennis skill, the athlete may find that swimming has upset him and the rugby place-kicker may wish he had not played a season's association football. The important word however is 'may'. Frequently there may be some interference but some benefit too. Thus it is probably better for the person who wishes to become an expert tennis player to play and practise tennis all the time if possible but, if he cannot, then playing other racket games may on balance be beneficial. Difficulties caused by interference can be overcome to a certain extent by reviewing the skill at intervals. After each successive review, forgetting occurs more slowly so that if a skill is 'overlearned' in the first place and then reviewed many times, the point is ultimately reached where the skill can be retained permanently with only very occasional practice periods.

The question of interference must be now examined further under the heading of transfer of training.

## (2) TRANSFER OF TRAINING

The problem of transfer is basic to educational procedure and it has already been mentioned from time to time in this book (for example, in pages 55–69) without the term transfer actually being used.

What effect does training in one task have on the learning and performance of another task? Unfortunately there is no easy answer to this question. Learning of a new physical activity may be speeded up, hindered or qualitatively changed by previous learning or it may not be affected at all.

When previous learning aids the new, then transfer is said to be positive. For example there is positive transfer when an individual who has learned to swim in salt water can immediately swim in fresh water even though the buoyancy is different, or when a person who has learned roller skating can acquire ice-skating skills more quickly than he would otherwise have done. When previous learning makes a new task more difficult to learn then transfer is said to be negative. Thus if a person took longer to acquire the skill of (say) discus-throwing after learning to shot-putt than he would have done before, then this would be a case of negative transfer. More often, however, an old skill causes interference but not negative transfer. This means that it temporarily impedes the new learning but still enables the skill to be acquired in a shorter time than would have been possible without the previous training. This interference usually occurs in the initial stages of acquiring a skill but it can also occur at a later stage. Thus the tennis player who turns to squash often makes speedy progress at the beginning but later on finds difficulties arising solely because of his skill in tennis. These difficulties do not mean however that he necessarily makes slower over-all progress than the beginner with the same innate ability who has not played any racket games or fives. Wolfle[154] refers to the experience of pilots who have no difficulty in learning to fly a new type of plane but may at a later date suffer interference, occasionally with disastrous results, when their reactions have become automatic. Readers may have had the same experience when transferring from an old to a new car with a different gear-box or the handbrake in a different place.

Interesting data, which show how complicated this question is, have been produced by Entwisle.[155] Persons who learned to drive in the same special school and who took a Ministry of Transport test were divided into two groups – those who had had previous experience on horse-vehicles (Group A) and those who had not (Group B). Those in Group A took less time to pass the test and had less failures than B, until they reached the age of forty. Thereafter their results were worse but it must be pointed out that the over forties were not only older but also had had much more horse-vehicle experience. The optimal transfer in learning to drive appeared to be with those who had had about three years' horse-vehicle experience.

When however the records of these drivers in normal employment were examined it was found that Group A had more accidents throughout. This might be due to the tendency for previously acquired habits to assert themselves in situations of emergency or stress. The older drivers in both groups had the lowest accident scores. The effects of previous training in this instance were obviously complex for the pattern in training was different from that on the job itself.

Sometimes, of course, previous learning has no effect and the one certain fact which emerges from the hundreds of experiments on transfer is that transfer of training is not automatic and that positive transfer cannot often be predicted with certainty.

In everyday practice the matter is often confused by the fact that training in an activity may build up strength, endurance and mobility and these may enable a person who tackles a new skill to start with a higher initial ability if the new skill requires these particular attributes. There is some doubt as to whether physical attributes of this kind do automatically transfer to new circumstances. It has been reported[156] that 'Morehouse described some experiments in which subjects did a simple elbow-flexing exercise, lifting a weight into positions – waist-level and above the head. A subject who trained at waist-level doubled his strength at that level but was no stronger at head-height although he was using exactly the same muscles in both cases'. Thus 'training a muscle may strengthen it for one task but not for another'. But even if transfer of strength, mobility and endurance does occur this is not transfer of training in the sense in which it is used here. Transfer of training refers to learning. Strength, endurance and mobility are not learned. Skill, however, is learned and therefore the question is whether training in one skill will affect the rate of learning another skill.

First let us examine a little of the evidence concerning transfer of training. Many experiments have been concerned with bilateral transfer or the transfer of a skill from one member of the body to another. For example Munn[157] gave his subjects fifty trials with the left hand at a game in which a wooden ball on the end of a string had to be flipped into a wooden cup. He then gave one group of subjects 500 trials with the right hand while the other group rested. Each group was then given another 50 trials with the left hand and the experimental group improved 61·14 per cent whereas the control group improved only 28·55 per cent. 'The average amount of transfer due to practice with the right hand was, therefore, 32·59 per cent.' Positive transfer has also been shown to occur between hand and foot. It may be of interest to record here that Karoly Takacs was world champion in rapid-fire pistol shooting before the war, lost his right arm during the war and yet won gold medals at the Olympic Games in 1948 and 1952 using his left hand.[158]

Then there have been experiments dealing with the transfer of patterns of movement from one situation to another. Seymour[159] says that 'when a certain level of performance has been attained on the component elements of a task, there is little loss when these are combined into the whole task' but Ungerson[160] comments critically on this and says that Seymour's 'most important basic assumption is relatively ill-founded'. In any case Seymour's view could only be applied to those few physical education skills in which the component elements are identical in the total task and are combined successively. This has already been discussed on pages 65–66.

Oliver[161] conducted an experiment on the value of standing breast-stroke land drill to children who had had no previous training or instruction in swimming and to children who were water-borne. The 88 children in the non-swimmers' group were from the first two years of primary school and the 83 children in the water-borne group were aged 9·8 to 13·8 years. All the children attended the baths for a half-hour lesson weekly from the same instructor and those in the experimental groups received in addition five minutes of land-drill practice during the normal physical training lessons which were held four times a week in the case of the non-swimmers and three times a week for the water-borne. In neither case was land drill found to make any significant contribution towards teaching the children to swim. On the other hand Minaert[162] found that a course in dry-ski-ing was advantageous to the beginning ski-er.

Egstrom, Logan and Wallis[163] found that practice with a light ball was as effective as practice with a heavier ball in developing skill to throw a heavier ball for accuracy with the non-preferred hand. Practice with the heavier ball when transferring to the lighter ball did not demonstrate a corresponding effect.

Although the authors make no such observation this is a further example of a principle already pointed out by Bartlett[164] when he says 'there is also some evidence that transfer is more likely to be made from the relatively difficult to the relatively easy than from the relatively easy to the relative difficult'. In the above experiment throwing with the heavier ball was the easier task judging by the scores made by the students taking part. The evidence to which Bartlett refers includes experiments by Welford and Szafran[165] into the throwing of chains at a target under three different conditions and by Gibbs[166] using a tracking task. The latter states that 'the ability to deal with difficult situations cannot be acquired in practising easy ones'. In all these cases the adjustments which had to be made involved the motor patterns to a major extent.

On the other hand Deese[167] mentions an experiment by Lawrence in which preliminary practice on an easy task produced greater transfer to a difficult task than preliminary practice on difficult material. In this experiment rats learned to discriminate between two boxes with a small difference in brightness more easily if in the preliminary training the brightness levels were quite different. Animals trained throughout on boxes where the brightness difference was small, found it difficult to solve the problem. This however is quite a different type of case. Here the problem was one of discovering the critical difference, and did not involve motor patterns to any great extent.

There are many examples of difficult to easy and also of easy to difficult transfer which have been summarized by Holding[168] and much further evidence is required before conclusions on this point can be drawn with any certainty. For the moment the indications are, as has already been pointed out in discussing whole and part methods (p. 59–69), that when a skill with difficult movement patterns is to be learned, it is better to work straight away on that skill rather than use lead-up practices, provided that the learner is mature enough to carry out the actions and does not get so discouraged that he gives up altogether. But if it is not the technique which is important but the ability to notice relevant external cues, and to understand the needs of the situation, then the solution to the problem may be more easily comprehended if the simpler case is dealt with first. This implies that tactical situations should be taught first in their simplest forms.

Transfer of training has so far been viewed in rather a specific way for similarity between two skills in patterns of movement or patterns of stimuli have formed the main basis to the discussion. But transfer can also occur in a more general way through the learning of certain attitudes of approach and ways of tackling new problems. It is possible to learn how to learn.

Experiments involving the transfer of principles must therefore be considered. The principles may be concerned with technique or with an appreciation of the problem or situation. An example of the former is the experiment by Colville described on page 29. She found that time spent on instruction in principles instead of practice was neither beneficial nor detrimental to transfer.

In the experiment by Hendrickson and Schroeder,[169] on the other hand, the principles were concerned with the theory of refraction and marksmanship was not involved. In this case knowledge of theory facilitated transfer and the theory is, as Judd has said,[170] 'a frame in which experiences may be properly held apart and at the same time together'. Cox's experiment described on pages 17–18 was extended to include a test of transfer to other operations involved in assembling and stripping an electric lamp-holder. The 'practisers' showed no reliable evidence of transfer from the container assembling operation to other operations, whereas the 'trainees' group showed a large net gain. In this case however the distinction which is here being made between principles concerning movements only and general principles was confused because the training given covered both.

How can these results regarding transfer be explained? At one time it was believed that certain subjects trained the mind. Thus it was supposed that a training in Classics developed the mind and not only fitted a person to cope with all sorts of other subjects but made good thinkers. This view is now believed by most people to be fallacious. Thus Thorndike[171] has said: 'The expectation of any large differences in general improvement of the mind from one study rather than another seems doomed to disappointment . . . When the good thinkers studied Greek and Latin; these studies seemed to make good thinking. Now that the good thinkers study Physics and Trigonometry, these seem to make good thinkers. If the abler pupils should all study Physical Education and Dramatic Art, these subjects would seem to make good thinkers. These were, indeed, a large fraction of the programme of studies for the best thinkers the world has produced, the Athenian Greeks. After positive correlation of gain with initial ability is allowed for, the balance in favour of any particular study is certainly not large.'

Sutcliffe and Canham[172] carried out some research into the effect of extra physical training lessons on boys. Eighty-four boys with an average age at the commencement of the experiment of 12 years 4 months were divided into three equivalent forms with a weekly distribution of lessons as shown in Table 10.

TABLE 10
WEEKLY DISTRIBUTION OF LESSONS

| Form | English | French | Maths | P.T. | Appreciation of Art | Music | B.B.C. |
|------|---------|--------|-------|------|-----|-------|--------|
| N | 5 | 5 | 5 | 2 | 0 | 0 | 0 |
| R | 4 | 4 | 4 | 2 | 1 | 1 | 1 |
| T | 4 | 4 | 4 | 5 | 0 | 0 | 0 |

The number of lessons in other subjects were alike for each form.

The results were summarized as follows: 'When a form has an extra lesson a week in each of the subjects English, French, and Mathematics it makes better progress than other forms which either do extra physical training or else spend extra time on "relief subjects". But when each form spends the same time on the three subjects then there is some indicaton that a form doing extra physical training makes better progress in academic subjects than a form which spends a correspondingly extra time on relief subjects.' The extra physical training had a marked effect on bodily improvement as measured by gymnastic type tests of flexibility and strength, but the results did not show that Form T had made any better progress in athletic activities such as running 50 yards and 440 yards, the standing high jump and strength of kick and throw.

Physical educationists however seem to have a tendency to make assumptions somewhat of this type. It often appears to be assumed that what is learned in the gymnasium will be transferred elsewhere. Thus Munrow talks[173] of 'physical wisdom' and Morison[174] of 'a pool of general skill'. though it should also be observed that both make their subsequent claims of transfer to the learning of physical skills with considerable diffidence. Certainly claims of this kind cannot be accepted uncritically. Certainly too there is no experimental evidence as yet to support the assumption that a training in movement will enable every individual to deal with situations in which movement is involved more satisfactorily than those who have had other types of training.

Transfer can best be explained on the grounds that it occurs to the extent that two situations are similar. This similarity may however occur in different ways. It may be the stimuli which are similar or it may be the responses or it may be that the same general principle governs both tasks. It must be remembered that the similarity is perceived by the learner and so it does not follow that the same transfers will occur in the case of every individual. Positive transfer is easier and more likely to occur when instruction is given; particularly if the teaching encourages the learner to be on the look-out for similarities and differences and if attention is drawn to underlying principles of wider application. Indeed Bartlett[175] has said that 'the most fundamental thing about transfer is that if it is desired it must, as a rule, be sought and prepared for in the style of instruction or teaching. So long as the emphasis is upon the particular material or problem that is to be studied the scales are weighted against any positive transfer. If stress is laid upon the principles of construction of the material or on the manner in which the components of a skill contribute to the task set, the balance is tipped in favour of the maximum positive transfer and the minimum interference'. It is because the 'practisers' in Cox's[176] experiments had not had appropriate instruction and the 'trainees' had, that positive transfer only occurred in the case of the latter. In some cases too the 'similarity' may be present because of the emotional attitude of the learner. For instance an individual who has met success in one ball game may approach another in such a way as to perceive likenesses. Again an individual who has been taught to look for generalizations or underlying principles is in a frame of mind favourable for the transfer of training.

The transfer may however have detrimental effects in certain circumstances. Thus where a new response is required to an old stimulus – as in driving a car with the handbrake in a different position – interference is likely. This is also so when two skills appear similar but in fact differ in some major respect. Siipola and Israel[177] have also suggested that most conflict is present in learning motor tasks when the two tasks are at about the same level of development and particularly when that level is of a low standard. This implies that an individual should not begin to learn skills which have some similarities at the same time. The teacher should therefore bear this in mind when arranging the athletic skills curriculum. For instance it would be preferable for a beginners' class in athletics to be taught dissimilar events such as running the half-mile and the high jump rather than two or three jumping events which are apparently some-what alike but which have subtle and important differences. It would be inadvisable for a group to begin to learn badminton and squash rackets or lawn tennis at the same time. The author has found that students beginning lawn tennis and athletics in the same summer term have experienced great difficulty in learning a forehand drive after a lesson in throwing the discus or in trying to throw the javelin immediately after being taught to serve. To avoid conflict it is better to reach a reasonable standard in one skill before commencing another skill which has some similarities. As a person gets more expert so can he learn to discriminate more easily between two skills which are at the same level of development and he can then avoid much of the interference.

It may then be concluded that transfer having beneficial effects may occur but that it is more likely when teaching of the right type is used. If any individual practises an activity without being encouraged to perceive relationships then his skill is likely to be highly specific to the situation in which it is practised. It is always advisable where possible for practice to be carried out in the general situation in which the skill is to be performed. If the skill has to be performed in a variety of situations then the individual must practise in a variety of situations.

If then an individual knows what skill he wishes to learn it is best for him to work on that skill rather than to do other activities and to hope that positive transfer will occur. Gymnastics may help an individual to play association football or hockey but if the individual wishes to be highly skilled at them it is more profitable for him to spend the time on football or hockey rather than on gymnastics.

In the light of the observations so far made on transfer, consideration should now be given to the ground on which claims may be made that educational gymnastics has 'carry over to other skill learning'.[178]

First of all it cannot be claimed that educational gymnastics develops a central factor of physical ability for many attempts have been made to isolate a general motor factor but without success. Suggestions that it develops 'body awareness' or 'kinaesthetic sensitivity' should also be accepted with caution for proof of the existence of one such factor common to all motor skills is still awaited.

Indeed investigations by Witte,[179] who identified 7 factors when she administered 33 tests of kinaesthesis to 100 college women, by Wiebe[180] and by others referred to by Scott,[181] support the hypothesis that kinaesthesis is a complex of many independent components and that it cannot be thought of as a general trait.

Even if there is a factor of kinaesthesis common to all motor skills its effect appears to be infinitesimal compared with other factors specific to any particular motor skill. Research indicates that skills are highly specific and, as has been seen, similar skills which are not identical can interfere with one another. It has been shown in various investigations that even after a certain amount of practice there is an absence of appreciable positive correlation between the scores in separate tests of motor skills.

Laban[182] writes that 'It is obvious that a person who has learnt to distinguish the feel of pressing and gliding in all their shades of intensity will be able to do the practical tasks in which transitions between these two efforts are involved incomparably better and easier than a person who has hitherto never experienced such feel consciously'. But the one certain thing which is known of transfer is that it cannot be predicted with certainty and therefore one cannot agree with Laban that transfer under these circumstances is obvious. Doubts in his claims in this direction are increased by his later statement that 'In general effort-training, the feel of the shades of effort expression is achieved without the use of tools or objects'. What experimental evidence there is makes it clear that transfer cannot be assumed or even expected in such a situation.

The claim however that educational gymnastics helps in the learning of new skills because of the attitude it develops in the learner appears much more likely. Each individual learns to solve problems in terms of his own physical abilities and limitations and this should be a useful attitude to carry over into many fields of physical activity. There is however also a danger in this attitude for an individual must not become too conscious of himself when he comes to the physical skills of games and sports. Thus when a person learns a new complex skill he may have to go through the stage of thinking of the actions of various parts of his body but when he is an expert the act itself is automatic and his mind is left free to concentrate on other matters. If for some reason the expert does become conscious of parts of his body then the skill often breaks down temporarily. Educational gymnastics must therefore beware (so far as skill acquisition is concerned) of making a person develop the habit of thinking too consciously of parts of the body and their movements and tensions. Skill in its final application must be outward-looking, concerning itself with results and the effect on the environment.

Transfer can also take place through an understanding of the fundamental principles of movement and the only question here is whether a knowledge of the principles defined by Laban are really helpful in the acquisition of all skills. Different people will have different views on this point.

It is probable that Corlett[183] best sums up the present view when she says: 'There is no proof that Modern Educational Gymnastics helps in the learning of a specific new skill. What is probably transferable is the attitude of mind, the approach to learning, a better prepared body and the ability to judge what sort of movement is required in a new situation.' Physical educationists should be continuously aware that description of a task does not necessarily enable one to predict whether transfer will occur or not, and that the nature and extent of the transfer of training in physical education remains to be investigated.

## (3) MOTIVATION

Since intensive and intelligent practice plays a major part in the ultimate standards achieved by any individual, motivation may be said to play a vital part in skill attainment. Effort can often overcome initial disadvantages in innate abilities or physiques. Under the heading of motivation may be discussed the wide variety of conditions which stimulate a person to action and direct his behaviour. These conditions may affect his performance or his rate of learning.

The effect of motivation has been shown by Schwab[184] who was investigating fatigue. He measured the time in seconds during which individuals could hang suspended from a bar and found that, on average, subjects hung on for more than twice as long if offered a money reward. Strong motivation prevented fatigue from affecting results so soon and performance was thus improved. Where a complex skill is concerned, however, very high motivation can sometimes affect performance detrimentally. The drive to win may be so great that tension is caused and the skill may break down. But unless a person experiences strong needs or drives it is unlikely that he will put in the effort and attention which is required to perform the activity to his maximum capacity nor to discover how to perform any particular skill to a high level in the first place. Since perfection is never reached in the complex skills with which this book is concerned, the drive to discover new solutions which improve on the old is important if progress is to continue. Responses must be discovered and practised and therefore motivation affects the level of skill which is reached and retained.

The conditions which may operate on any one individual at any particular time are many and varied. Some of these 'drives' such as hunger and thirst are unlearned but many are learned and these may be greatly affected by the attitudes of other people and particularly teachers and parents. In present-day society, for example, material goals loom large and the need to be recognized as 'good' at something has become more intense. Drives which have developed through experience can be very difficult to change but there are great differences in this between different people and different drives. Sometimes when a goal which an individual has been trying to reach for many years is removed or suddenly comprehended as unattainable, the individual's personality may be vitally affected and changed.

What are the conditions which drive a person to physical activity and which direct his interests to the acquisition of a physical skill? Any discussion of this problem must owe a great deal to Burnett and Pear[185] and in the following pages their work has been drawn on extensively. First of all it does seem that a certain amount of muscular exercise is a primary need in any human being. In play and especially in activities which exercise the kinaesthetic and cutaneous organs the individual enjoys the movements because of the pleasant physical feelings and physical satisfaction which he gets. In many physical activities and particularly in some forms of dance the simple or complex skill patterns are closely related to instinctive patterns of movement and to natural rhythms. A person's interest in the pleasure which he derives from his kinaesthetic sensation is a motive force which has been called 'muscular sensuousness' by Burnett and Pear. The goal here is the immediate one of participation and might be termed intrinsic motivation since what the individual does or learns is solely for the sake of engaging in the activity itself. Play enables the individual to find out about himself and his environment, helps him to satisfy his curiosity and widen his perceptions.

Play also enables him to develop control of himself, of other people and of objects. The greater the skill which he succeeds in developing, the more delight he will have in feeling power over himself. Thus the climber meets the challenge of the mountains, the yachtsman the tests of wind and tide and the dancer the problems of self-expression. More than skill alone may be involved; it may also be necessary to learn to control the emotions under stress. The boxer or rugby footballer learns to control himself when hurt, the mountaineer does not lose his head in difficult circumstances, the games player or athlete tries not to let his nervousness upset his performance. Individuals may also experience pleasure in feeling power over others, as is possible in combative sports and in some games, or over animals as in riding.

The need to feel power has been called the mastery or self-assertion motive. It is important to recognize the need which most people have for achievement of *some* kind, a need to prove themselves, to feel that they are as good as others. In our society which tends to hold back young people – and as the numbers of old increase the chances for promotion at work are likely to decrease – physical recreation is one field in which the young can prove themselves. Achievement or 'success' even on a minor scale in any one activity tends to give an individual more stability. This success is in terms of each individual's goal and public competition is not necessarily involved. An individual may get satisfaction of this motive by canoeing down a river or by going a long walk across the moors or by a mastery of movement for self-expression as in dance. But for many the satisfaction of the self-assertion motive is best obtained in highly competitive situations and particularly in games and sports where the individual is against all the others. Where this motive is very strong it may be known as the 'killer instinct'. An individual with considerable skill may prove to be a poor team player if this motive of self-assertion is too strong and even in individual sports he may spoil the game for his opponent. It is no pleasure for instance to play squash rackets with such a person.

The good team player has to like competition but he also has to enjoy co-operating with others. Many persons who do not like playing for themselves can fight very hard for their own team which seems to them to be greater than the individual. In dancing, 'keep-fit', and in some forms of gymnastic work, group feeling can be developed and enjoyed. Many people need too the approbation of others – their friends or teachers or the public – or they may simply need friendship which often arises in the social atmosphere of a sports club.

Muscular sensuousness and satisfaction of the need for mastery may be increased for some people if danger is involved. Many physical activities such as climbing, sailing, ski-ing and horse-jumping are exciting because of the risks which have to be taken; and to overcome the fear and escape from the dangers implies greater skill.

Play is normally a means of relaxation for it enables the older person to withdraw for a time from the worries of everyday life. But although games and sports can be a relief from the frustrations of life they also provide their own frustrations. Anyone who has been in a golf club will be aware of this! An individual may also on occasions take up a particular activity as a substitute gratification for some desire which has been frustrated because its outcome is not socially acceptable. Thus a pugnacious person may sublimate his pugnacity by taking part in boxing, wrestling, judo or rugby football.

Frequently an activity taken up in the first place for whatever reason, becomes an end in itself. It creates its own interest and motivation. But this is not always so for sometimes a person finds that the novelty has worn off and the drive to take part is no longer present. This may be because the goal which the individual sets himself is easily attained or it may be that it is set so high that he suddenly realizes he cannot achieve it and so gives up. Hall[186] says: 'Audiences swell to watch the experts, and as the "stars" grow in brilliance the spectators are frozen to inactivity by their growing sense of ineptitude. Not every activity invites attempts to action; only those which appear within the possible scope of the spectator tempt him.' The level of aspiration of a learner is important for it has been found that the good student is the one who tends to set a level of aspiration just a little above past achievement. He therefore gets the satisfaction of attaining his goal but he then immediately raises his sights. Teachers can probably help children to get into the habit of doing this. It means that the ladder of success must have many rungs and the child must be made aware of his achievements and encouraged to see the next step and to realize that he can attain it.

Judo with its belt system has such a ladder built into its organization but whether the rungs are placed at the right distances apart is obviously open to argument. In activities such as swimming and athletics there are many different systems of standards which can be used to encourage the less able children. Those standards which take into account age, height, and weight tend to be more satisfactory than those based on age alone, particularly in the case of boys. Shann[187] has re-reported a method of organizing school athletics which sets out to give encouragement to every boy. The boys are grouped according to McCloy's[188] formula: 20 times age plus 6 times height plus weight. Points can be gained (a) by achieving Standards (b) for championship positions (c) according to the position of the individual in the whole school and (d) for Athletic Quotients.[188] Every performance therefore receives recognition by the award of points and so every effort may be seen by the boy to be worthwhile. Achievement scales such as those drawn up by Cozens, Trieb and Nielson[189] can also be used as an incentive for children at all levels of attainment.

Mace[190] has pointed out that since activities which are too easy pall and those which are too difficult are abandoned in despair, the popularity of a game seems to depend in part on determining the optimum degree of difficulty conducive to maximum satisfaction. He suggests that the 'optimum is itself a moving point on the scale of performance from the early to the late stages of practice and might perhaps be best defined in terms of the percentage improvement to be aimed at'. Should then the rungs of the ladder of success get closer together as it becomes more difficult to make any apparent progress?

The experimental results of Gebhard[191] have shown that the attractiveness of an activity is determined not only by past experience of success or failure but also by expectation of future success or failure. Cartwright[192] has found some indication that anticipation of failure reduces attractiveness more than the actual experience of failure and that 'a person's view of the future is the primarily decisive factor in producing changes in attractiveness. Past failure does not always lead to an expectation of future failure'. Cartwright also found that the conception of failure not only affected the particular activity concerned but also spread to other activities which the learner viewed as being of the same type. Thus failure in a ball game may make a child dislike all ball games, or all physical activity or even all school work, depending on the way the child categorizes the activity. A teacher should therefore make sure that he takes no action which will make a child anticipate failure.

On the other hand, provided there is genuine hope of progress, immediate achievement is not necessary. Thus Allport[193] says: 'It seems to be neither the perfected talent nor the automatic habit that has driving power, but the imperfect talent and the habit-in-the-making . . . The active motive subsides when its goal is reached, or in the case of a motor skill, when it has become at last automatic.

'. . . Now, in the case of the permanent interests of personality, the situation is the same. A man whose motive is to acquire learning, or to perfect his craft, can never be satisfied that he has reached the end of his quest, for his problems are never completely solved, his skill is never perfect.' In the author's view an individual is unlikely to reach the top in any game or sport if his motivation does not include the need to try to perfect his skill for its own sake. An individual with this drive can never be satisfied and in only rare instances is he likely to be happy with his performance. Walker[194] has perhaps put the point appropriately when he writes: 'I played football because I had an inner compulsion to do so. Nothing else mattered. Fame, fortune – I never considered these. It was the game that mattered and for it I was prepared from the earliest days **to** risk my health, my schooling, my hopes of marriage, and eventually, a considerable business career.

'If you find this hard to believe, then, simply, you haven't got it; I mean you haven't got the bug that eats at a man with as much virulence as the drink-bug and the gambling-bug and the drug-bug eat at other men.

'If you've got it, you've got it, and that's an end of it.'

Extrinsic motivation in which the goals are extraneous to the activity are also important drives to some people. Approbation by the public has already been mentioned but it must not be assumed that all public performers desire or court public praise. Often to compete in public is the only way in which a highly skilled performer can try out his skill. Elliott[195] has said: 'If I had my chance I would run my races and win gold medals without being in the public eye. You've got to pay the price for these things and the price is being in the public eye.' Economic drives also increasingly tend to play a part. But economic drives make play into work. If an activity has to be performed when the individual is getting no enjoyment from it then it may be called work and economic needs drive a person to do this.

The motivation of any one person at any one time will be made up of a whole variety of conditions but certain needs will tend to be the dominant ones. But the ones which are dominant may change. Thus one of the writer's students stated that he first interested himself in swimming because it was a challenge – he had to overcome fear and master himself in order to swim at all. Then he found that he obtained what might be termed pure enjoyment from the activity itself. Then he began to desire to perfect his ability and as his skill improved he began to get ambitious and wish to defeat others competitively. Having reached a high level he then found that he no longer enjoyed swimming as much as he had done previously and even sometimes disliked it. He continued with it however because he felt that he would have wasted so much time and effort if he did not do so and because he felt that he would be giving in because he had not quite achieved the goal he had set himself. Social considerations were also involved for his friends were in swimming and having spent so much time on this activity he had not developed other interests or groups of friends.

Elliott[196] has said: 'At some time or another you come to a point of no return. You've given up so much to achieve your goal and even when you've realized it, it would be stupid to throw away all that work and sacrifice – that's why I wouldn't like to retire now. I have done so much to get here that it would be silly to give it all away at this stage of the game. I think I'll go on for as long as I can.'

It is however more difficult to hang on to a position once one's goal has been achieved because fear of losing one's place rather than fun begins to become the main drive. In activities like lawn tennis, cricket and association football this can have disastrous effects. The individual begins to play with a different mental attitude. He is concerned not to lose rather than to win and his play becomes unadventurous and defensive. This is one of the reasons why the newspapers can do so much harm to a young sportsman. If they build him up in the public eye on the basis of one or two good performances he tends to get an inflated idea of his own excellence. Similarly if he gets selected for an international before he has truly earned his place. Then, if he does not win and the newspapers or people he meets or the selectors seem to suggest that he ought to have done so, he begins to get afraid of losing. Instead therefore of continuing to increase the number of his skills, of experimenting and playing to win, he begins to play safe and to cut out of his repertoire those skills which are less reliable. This is particularly true in tennis where people often seem to take an unnecessary amount of notice of the score, and thus it may seem to pay to just lose to two people rather than beat one and lose 6–0, 6–0 to the other. The number of junior champions, particularly girls, and others of promise who are faced with such a learning 'dilemma' is large particularly in the present set-up where being young is made unduly important. The learner is faced with a confusing situation. He is perhaps eighteen and has been junior champion and everyone expects great things of him. Then he happens to lose to another junior. From then on every time he plays someone he thinks (often wrongly) is less good than himself, he suffers agonies fearing he may lose. As a result he often does lose but to change his outlook is difficult because the changed situation resembles the one with which he is familiar. Sometimes the learner will go on in this way for some time and ultimately he will either give up altogether or change his goals and thus never fully develop his potential. Sometimes the fact that people lose interest in him enables him to get on 'an even keel' again and perceive the changes necessary to meet the situation.

Much motivation is learned and therefore the actions of others can seriously affect the type of interests and goals that any one individual develops. Teachers particularly have responsibility in this field. If it is believed that physical recreation is important then care should be taken to build up in every individual the desire to take part in some physical activity. It is perhaps more a case of not destroying the drives already present, for most young children enjoy physical activity and want to learn. It is later on in school and in adult life that many people lose interest. Is this a natural result of growing up in present-day society or is it due in any way to what goes on in schools? To what extent do we play down the need for muscular exercise by publicizing the educational aspects of physical education or by making games and physical education the time which can be most easily sacrificed to academic work in the upper forms of the grammar schools? How far do we decrease the pleasure of the less able who need special help in the initial stages of skill acquisition, by giving the special coaching to those who are likely to represent the school in teams? To what extent do we try to meet the needs of every individual remembering that everyone will be different and that each person must be able to discover the effectiveness of his activity? How often have we helped a child, particularly a less able one, to build up a strong enough interest in a physical activity to cause him to make the effort to continue with it when he leaves school? As Commins and Fagin[197] have said 'providing suitable consequences is in many respects the key to the art of teaching. It is often the most neglected'.

Certain general rules about these 'consequences' could be laid down. First every individual should be encouraged to set goals which are within his reach but not too easily attainable. Secondly he should at all times have some measure of his effectiveness. Thirdly when he reaches his goal he should for a short time be allowed to get real pleasure from its attainment but then a new goal in accordance with his underlying drives should be set for him. After a time he should be encouraged to set himself this type of programme. Persons who select for teams have a great responsibility in building up a person's skill. They should make it clear on what grounds selection is made and they should then truly select on this basis. A person who is selected before he has reached the requisite standard, has attained his goal before he is ready for it. In his heart he will know that he cannot take a further step for a long time and so frequently satisfies himself with his present achievement and makes no further effort. Again if a person is selected before he has reached the requisite standard it has a bad effect on all those who have – for they get discouraged – and also on the group immediately below that standard. The latter group seeks out the reason why the person was selected and may come up with all sorts of different answers – favouritism, the individual 'looks good', potentiality not present ability, and so on. Having decided on a particular reason any individual whose goal is team selection will act accordingly. Thus instead of working on their skills with the aim of getting results, they may start to cultivate the 'right' people or they may build up skills which are noticeable or potentially good or are the ones recommended by some particular teacher – and so on. Again if an individual is not selected for a team when he is truly ready for it he will continue to try for a length of time which will depend on the strength of his motivation. Ultimately however if the goal is not achieved he is likely to try to reach it by other methods than those of genuine effort or to withdraw altogether or to change his goal to something which he can attain.

It is not however suggested that extraneous rewards of this kind should become the main driving force for participation in physical activity. They are only helpful or harmful aids, depending on how they are used. The teacher should aim to strengthen the conditions which appear to be present in most young children – the need for a certain amount of muscular exercise and self-expression and the drive to learn and to achieve. The adolescent and adult should still feel the need of physical exercise of some kind so that he is dissatisfied whenever he does not succeed in getting it and pleased when he does. This pleasure will be reinforced if he is also skilful in some activity and interested in developing that skill. As Munrow has said[198] 'through skill, there is likely to be a more permanent satisfaction and interest in physical activity'.

# VII

## MECHANISMS INVOLVED IN SKILL

A CONSIDERABLE amount is known about the structures of the nervous system and for a complete account readers should consult standard works[199] in physiology. This chapter brings in only those points which seem to the author to have a direct bearing on skill acquisition. Theories concerning the mechanisms of learning are still largely speculative and the views of various authorities[200] have been drawn on extensively.

The events which can be observed in any skilled act may be divided into the sensory and the motor or, if a machine analogy is used, the input and output.

*Input*

The information from stimuli both outside and inside the individual is conveyed through the sensory nerves from the sense organs or receptors, which act as receiving instruments or indicators. These sense organs which are stimulated and initiate reactions in the living person are specialized as they are each highly sensitive only to one particular kind of stimulus. For example, in the human skin there are specific receptors related to sensations of heat, others related to cold, others again to pain, touch and so on.

Receptors are of three kinds depending on where they are situated. Thus they may be classified into exteroceptors, interoceptors and proprioceptors. The first two will not be dealt with in any detail because any elementary textbook in physiology covers them adequately. Suffice it to say that the exteroceptors receive stimuli from outside the organism and include the receptor cells of the eye (there are about 120 million sensory elements in the retina alone), and of those parts of the ear concerned with hearing. The interoceptors receive stimuli from the alimentary tract and lungs. The proprioceptors are mainly located within the muscles, tendons and joints giving rise to the muscle or kinaesthetic sense but also include those receptors associated with the vestibular organs of the ear. Proprioception is one of the most highly developed and complex senses.

The sensory information known as kinaesthetic which arises from the movements of muscles, tendons and joints involves at least three different kinds of receptors. There are those receptors associated with the muscles which are stimulated by the stretching of the muscle, those around the ends of the tendons which are stimulated by contraction, and those in the joints which include corpuscles generally considered to convey information relating to subcutaneous pressure.

Kinaesthesis gives knowledge of position as well as of movement. Apart from this however there is sensory information concerning motion and position from the vestibular organs of the ear and this helps the individual to keep his balance. The semi-circular canals are the chief receptors for rotational movements since they are affected by angular accelerations. There is some evidence that they are also stimulated to some degree by position and linear acceleration. The utricular otolith organs respond to gravity and to linear accelerations.

In 1826 Charles Bell[201] wrote that 'between the brain and the muscles, there is a circle of nerves; one nerve conveys the influence from the brain to the muscle; and another gives the sense of the condition of the muscle to the brain'. The proprioceptive system is then important in determining posture and movements. Proprioceptors have recently been defined by Lissman[202] as 'sense organs capable of registering continuously deformations (changes in length) and stresses (tensions, compressions) in the body. These can arise from the animal's own movements, or may be due to its weight, or to other external mechanical forces. Through their activity the proprioceptors help to establish the relationship of each part of the body to the rest and of the body as a whole to the outside world'.

It should be clear from this brief description of input that when one talks of the 'feel' of a movement the mechanisms involved may be many and varied. Sensory organs in the skin, in the muscles, tendons and joints, and in the vestibular organs of the ear may all be concerned. Kinaesthesis alone can include sensory information from at least three sources. It is therefore inadvisable at our present stage of knowledge to make statements about training the kinaesthetic sense and indeed such statements may prove grossly misleading.

*Output*

The effector organs are the muscles and glands. There are three classes of muscles known as striped, smooth and heart muscles. The smooth muscles occur in the visceral organs of the body and their normal response is slow and rhythmic. The heart muscles also contract rhythmically and rather faster than the smooth ones. The striped muscles contract most speedily and move the body and its limbs by exerting forces on the bony levers of the skeleton. The muscle fibres involved in movement contract to their maximal extent if the stimulation is enough to make them act at all. This principle is often referred to as the 'all or none' law. The strength of any contraction therefore depends on the number of fibres in the muscles which are stimulated sufficiently to contract. The glands are specialized organs which when stimulated produce chemical products which affect body functioning. Perhaps the most interesting glands in connection with physical performance are the adrenals which when stimulated secrete adrenalin into the blood producing the heightened activity and keyed-up state which accompanies an 'emergency' reaction of an individual. Again more detailed information on the effector organs should be obtained from standard works.

Now that the input and output mechanisms have been briefly described it is necessary to consider the transmission system which connects them.

All sense organs or receptors are associated with the peripheral endings of afferent nerve fibres or neurones which pass from the periphery to the central nervous system. All effectors are associated with efferent nerve fibres which pass from the central nervous system to the muscles and glands. When a neurone is stimulated the stimulus may be too weak to arouse the fibre at all. If however it is strong enough to arouse any response then the maximal response of which the fibre is capable at that particular time is made and the resultant impulse known as an action potential passes along the nerve fibre. The impulse consists of a change of state in the fibre which is both chemical and electrical in nature and passes along the neurone at a rate which varies according to the diameter of the neurone and other physical factors but which in any one fibre is always the same. The speed of conduction varies between about 2 and 200 m.p.h. A small period of time (the latent period) must therefore always elapse between the application of a stimulus and the response of a muscle. When an impulse has passed there is a very short period known as the refractory phase during which further stimulation of the fibre has no effect. A very strong and sustained stimulus will thus cause a succession of impulses to pass along a fibre with a length of time equal to the refractory phase between each impulse whereas an intermittent stimulus will cause the impulses to follow one another at longer time intervals.

A very strong stimulus will also involve more fibres in the carrying of the message. Nervous messages associated with sensory and motor functions are essentially alike in that there are no differences in the quality or nature of the impulse. There are differences in the frequency of the impulses depending on the intensity of stimulation and as the nerve fibres are collected in bundles called nerves the number of neurones firing in any particular nerve can also vary, particularly since some of the larger nerves of the body contain both afferent and efferent fibres and both somatic and autonomic types.

The activity of the nerve is the sum of the activity of the individual neurones making up the nerve. Since the neurones may differ in their conduction rates and refractory periods, they can discharge at different rates which means that the response of the whole nerve may well be continuous.

Messages from the afferent neurones pass to the efferent neurones by way of the central nervous system which consists of the spinal cord and the brain. The messages from the central nervous system to the skeletal muscles are carried by the somatic motor nerve system and those to the muscles controlling the internal organs of the body by the autonomic nervous system.

The simplest possible system of transmission was that envisaged by the classical conception of the reflex arc. Here the stimulus from the environment was received by a receptor and the information was passed along the ingoing sensory nerve fibre across a junction point known as the synapse to the outgoing motor nerve fibre which activated the muscle fibres. The connexion at the synapse was by contact and was located in the spinal cord. Diagrammatically this can be represented as in Fig. 12.

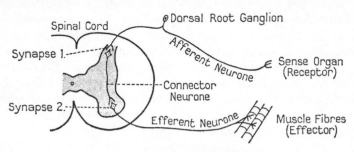

FIG. 12. Diagram of a reflex arc.

This very simple form of reflex arc never occurs on its own in human beings, although the knee-jerk reflex is basically of this type. It is however complicated by the fact that every sensory fibre is connected not with one motor fibre but with several. Every motor fibre is also connected with several sensory fibres and so multiple synapses are present. This means that there is not just one nervous 'pathway' along which the message can travel but many. A volley of impulses from one sensory organ may therefore affect many motor neurones. For example if a person is rotated to the right for a while and then asked to stand with arms outstretched and offer no voluntary resistance, the results of the impulses from the vestibular apparatus of the ear are widespread. 'The head then turns to the right (compensatory deviation), as do the trunk and arms, the left arm rises while the right is lowered and there is a tendency for the left leg to extend, the right to flex. The resulting position has been described as that of a discus thrower'.[203] Similarly impulses from many sensory fibres may connect with one motor neurone. These influences may alter excitation and therefore strengthen or inhibit the response; the knee-jerk for instance can be strengthened by clenching the fist.

Another complication to the classical conception of the reflex arc is that in the human being the impulses do not simply pass from receptor to effector by way of the spinal cord. Although the act is apparently carried out in this way and consciousness is not a necessary accompaniment, the person can nevertheless be aware that the act has happened. Indeed if he knows some-one is going to tap his leg to make the knee jerk he can reduce its effect by tensing other muscles in his leg. It is therefore clear that there is also some connexion with the brain via the spinal cord.

The spinal cord therefore not only provides many connexions between sensory and motor neurones but it also contains many nerves leading to and from the brain. The brain contains about 10,000,000,000 neurones and consists of three main parts: the brain stem which is an enlarged continuation of the spinal cord, the cerebellum and the cerebrum. All parts are probably involved in voluntary activity. Certain definite areas of the cerebral cortex are concerned with sense impressions from defined parts of the body and other specific areas are concerned with the movement of particular parts of the musculature. According to Ruch[204] however 'there is a growing tendency to think, not of distinct sensory and motor areas, but of a paracentral sensorimotor area'.

It can be seen from Fig. 13 that the vertical extent of particular sensory areas is not related to the area of skin represented. For example there is a larger area concerned with sensations from the foot than there is from the trunk. Similarly in the case of the motor representation, 'the area of the cortical field for a given body segment varies with the discreteness and variety of movement of that segment, not with the muscular mass involved'.[205] Thus the area devoted to the hand is many times greater than that concerned with the trunk. It must not be thought however that muscles are represented in the motor cortex. The motor area is organized in such a way that cells directing a particular movement are collected within one area and so a part of a muscle involved in many different movements will actually be represented many times and diffusely in the cortex. The cerebellum and the motor areas of the cerebrum

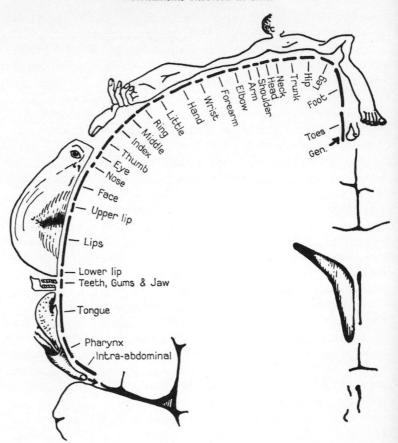

Fig. 13. Sensory Homunculus. The right side of the figurine is laid upon a cross section of the hemisphere and is drawn approximately in proportion to the extent of the sensory cortex devoted to it. The length of the underlying black lines indicates more accurately the comparative extent of each representation. The motor cortex presents the same general distribution of function. From W. Penfield and T. Rasmussen, *The Cerebral Cortex of Man*, Macmillan, New York, 1957.

are connected with each other and both exert a control over the muscles of the body. One of the main jobs of the cerebellum appears to be as a proprioceptive centre involved in the maintenance of posture, balance and steadiness of muscular action. It is believed to act as a regulator for if the cerebellum is destroyed no type of voluntary movement is lost but it is altered in character. People suffering from disorders of the cerebellum have great difficulty in co-ordinating voluntary movements. They may have poor muscle tone, difficulty in timing the components of movement and difficulty in making accurate changes of rate, direction and force. Gross oscillation of a limb in carrying out a movement is almost certainly due to cortical motor activity which is not being satisfactorily regulated by the cerebellum.

In a skilled act the cerebrum and cerebellum therefore act together. In carrying out a vault for example the decision to act and the direction of the trained skill comes from the cerebrum, the cerebellum co-ordinating postural adjustments and the steadiness of the movement. It should not however be supposed that there are specialized regions of the brain for particular motor capacities. In skilled acts requiring long and specialized training and concentration a large part of the brain seems to be involved.

At this stage it is advisable to distinguish between different types of movement. First there are the multitude of reflex actions which must be basic to many neuro-muscular activities. These do not normally involve the cerebrum though the mind may exercise some control over them if necessary. Weiss[206] has argued that 'the basic patterns of co-ordination arise by self-differentiation within the nerve centres, prior to, and irrespective of actual experience in their use'. If this is true, and Weiss has produced a great deal of experimental evidence to support his view, then every individual will have a repertoire of movement patterns which develop fully without practice as maturation takes place.

Then there are voluntary actions in which attention is given to the actual movement and in which the cerebrum is therefore involved. A learner of activities in physical education or physical recreation normally goes through a stage in attaining a skill when his conscious attention is given to the impressions received through the exteroceptors and particularly to those from the eye. Later on proprioceptive information is used and gradually the movement drops out of consciousness or becomes 'automatic'. If attention is focused on a movement and consideration is given to the limb or part of the body involved in that movement then it may be called 'planned'.[207] Neilsen says 'a planned act is first visualized as a motion or set of motions of the body musculature or of the parts of the body and, if he can see, the person uses his vision to guide the movement . . . A visual picture, essentially a motion picture, is then conceived.' The automatic act which comes about after practise of a planned movement, is set in motion by another part of the brain but the act is still 'supervised' in the sense that 'if an error occurs it is correlated by an ideational motor plan'.

The description so far given of the mechanisms does not take us very far. What we wish to know is how the sensory events result in the corresponding motor events and how skill is acquired. This indeed is a very difficult question and no final satisfactory answer has yet been given.

An early idea was that the nervous system was like a telephone system. When a stimulus was applied to a sense organ a transmission of some kind took place through a series of connexions and if suitably routed, caused the appropriate response to be made. The central nervous system thus acted as a kind of switchboard. This is probably quite a helpful picture of some parts of the nervous system for messages of an electrical nature are transmitted along sensory nerve fibres to motor nerve fibres via the central nervous system of the spinal cord and brain. But the idea that the function of the nervous system is merely one of conduction is not an adequate one.

In the first place there are systems in the body which are rhythmic in nature and which never rest. Respiration is a case in point. In the brain too it has been shown that some electrical activity is going on continuously and that nerve cells are active even when the individual is asleep. This rhythmicity which occurs in various parts of the nervous system independently of sensory information, must be self-maintaining and a system of this kind clearly differs from a reflex centre which is merely concerned with reflecting messages. The nervous system is not simply a passive one which comes to rest when unstimulated and the brain does not act merely as a switchboard for it 'is an organ whose activities literally control and dominate our life'.[208]

At any one time a multitude of stimuli are being received by the central nervous system from both outside and inside the individual. Some of these impulses cause activity and others inhibit it. Some arrive all the time so that there is a 'tonic' background, others only when there is some sensory change. It has already been pointed out that multiple synapses are the rule and this means that sensory impulses can interact so that changes in the environment can 'be reacted to not merely as a series of isolated intensity changes but as a whole pattern'.[208] A system of this kind is obviously variable and will therefore not always react in the same way to any particular sensory change.

Thus a man ski-ing down the same slope several times may react quite differently on each occasion to a ridge in the terrain or to a change in the snow surface. Again when in a slalom race he may on occasions never notice the audience at all but at other times they may impinge on his consciousness and distract his attention. A man shooting for goal may sometimes be affected by the cameramen at the side of the goal-posts and sometimes not. The same act of exhibitionism repeated by one particular individual may each time call forth quite different responses in another person.

A person then does not react so much to individual stimuli as to the pattern of stimuli which he perceives. It is important to distinguish between sensing a thing and perceiving it. Perception involves the interpretation of sense impressions. At the cinema a series of still pictures is seen or sensed but movement is perceived. A miler who has just passed the others up the back straight will have gained visual and possibly auditory impressions of the state of his opponents and he will have proprioceptive information about himself. He will thus be in a position to perceive his chances of winning. Whether he makes a correct interpretation or not will depend on how well he has managed to organize the sense impressions coming to him through so many different sensory channels. When a boxer receives a severe blow an inexperienced opponent may sense that he is hurt and that now is the time to put on the pressure whereas an experienced man may perceive that he is 'foxing'. This difference in perceptive ability arises through experience.

Stimuli then are integrated and grouped in such a way that some are selected as important and others are more or less ignored. What is perceived by any one individual will depend on this organizing process and also on his past actions and experiences. Every individual will be different and there will therefore be as many interpretations of any set of external stimuli as there are people. The organizing process of any one person will be limited by his inherited characteristics and influenced by his previous experiences. His interpretation will affect not only his present but also his future actions for he will anticipate on the basis of his perceptions. Exactly how all this is done is not known.

Another objection then to the telephone system analogy is that, in Welford's[209] words, 'each new perceptual response leaves the observer different from what he was before, so that the "past" which he brings to deal with any new stimulus is in some way changed . . . The past experience brought to deal with any incoming stimulus seems not to consist of any aggregate of past impressions, but appears to exist in an organized or schematized form which is affected by each new impression in a manner which can be compared to the modification of a "plastic" model'.

This concept has important implications in skill learning for it means that a person does not collect new experiences and add them to ones already in his possession, nor can he ever start anew with, so to speak, a clean slate. It is for this reason that early learning is so important. The framework established initially affects subsequent perception and therefore learning. The importance of good form from the start has already been stressed. The individual should also be in a fit state to learn. There is evidence for instance that learning when tired may affect subsequent performance levels. Results of two experiments[210] which were conducted on civilian air crew suggested strongly that 'the impaired performances of subjects meeting tasks for the first time when they are tired tend to be repeated on meeting the task for a second time when they are fresh, probably owing to the fixation of an inadequate method when fatigued'.

In the lower organisms changes in the external environment play the major part in determining their actions but the human being will react quite differently on different occasions to the same situation and internal organization is therefore of greater importance in his case. The elusive factor of motivation may greatly influence his responses and, as has been pointed out, previous experience and learning determine what he perceives and therefore how he acts.

The brain clearly permits retention of some trace of the effects of previous sensation but it is not known how this is done. A major difficulty in trying to solve the problem is that frequently, if the part of the cortical areas crucial to a particular motor function is destroyed, the motor function can gradually be recovered by the individual concerned. In other words the function is lost by the injury but the individual can relearn if the destruction is not too great. Thus the motor act in the uninjured individual appears to be retained in a particular area for when this is destroyed the act is lost. But the brain apparently can learn again so it presumably can substitute another part for the one which has been destroyed. Lashley[211] takes the view that recovery of functions depends upon reorganization of the nervous tissue remaining in the system concerned with the function. This means that motor functions can be recovered provided part of the motor system in the brain remains intact. There does not therefore seem to be any simple localization of function and, as the individual is able to select what shall be retained on the basis of results, the brain cannot be compared to a tablet on which impressions are made. 'The learning capacity of the nervous system is much more than a mere passive plasticity of a highly impressionable tissue. It is more comparable to the active functional ability of a complex machine.'[212]

The old idea that 'traces' of experiences exist in the brain so that memory can be compared to a series of photographs or gramophone records has given way to the suggestion that the brain remembers in the same kind of way as an electronic digital computer stores information. In this machine the information is retained not by an alteration in structure nor in any one particular place but in the form of electrical impulses circulating in circuits. As the brain consists of such a very large number of cells it may indeed be a fruitful idea to get away from dealing with one or two cells and try rather to consider memory in terms of collections of cells operating together.

Many new ways of looking at the nervous system and particularly the brain have been opened up by engineering developments and machines have been produced which behave in some way similarly to an animal or a human being.

For example, a type of machine which seems to exemplify some parts of human behaviour is one in which a form of automatic control or servo-mechanism is incorporated. A simple example of a control device is the thermostat. When the water in a tank reaches a certain temperature the thermostat automatically turns off the heating and then when the water temperature falls to a lower level it automatically turns the heat on again. The thermostat controls the output of the system so that the temperature of the water stays within a definite range. This is an example of negative feedback.

Now the hypothesis has been advanced that negative feedback mechanisms underlie the working of the central nervous system. It will be remembered that Bell (see page 125) suggested the 'circle of nerves' concept. Many circular pathways within the nervous system have since been shown to exist and some feedback loops have been demonstrated. When an act is being carried out information can be sent back by means of these closed loops. As Haldane[213] puts it 'the muscle fibres are not slaves who cannot answer back'. The output can therefore influence the input and thereby in turn exercise some control over the output. During a skilled movement of the arm, sense impressions are being sent back to the brain from the limb and these can be used to regulate the movement provided it is not a very speedy one as it is being made. When errors are occuring the negative feedback can operate continuously to compensate for them and thus the output can be corrected. Many movements are capable of modification in this way.

Time factors are, however, vital. In the first place when two stimuli occur in quick succession the response to the second stimulus is sometimes unduly long. Vince[214] and Craik[215] have produced examples where half a second had to elapse between two successive stimuli if normal and appropriate responses were to be made with any certainty. Secondly in the nervous system the maximal rate of conduction is slow enough to make time factors critically important. There are therefore many movements which are so fast that they cannot be modified when they are in process. Oldfield[216] reports that as a result of many experiments Vince came to the conclusion that 'sensory feedback plays a diminishing role in movements lasting less than 0·6 seconds and none in those lasting less than 0·4 seconds'. In such movements much of the data received may however be used to anticipate the trend and make adjustments on the basis of expectations. Much of the continuous feedback from muscles, tendons and joints operates at levels below consciousness. Indeed the body is equipped with many servo-mechanisms which can operate without the intervention of the cerebrum. For further discussion of these views vide Gibbs,[217] Walter[218] and Sluckin.[219]

Another approach to an understanding of the central nervous system has arisen as a result of the development of information theory. In any communication system there is a transmitter fed by the communication source, a receiver which passes the communication to its destination and a communication channel which links transmitter and receiver. The messages are received against a background of noise from the external environment and from inside the transmitter and receiver, and the information which is communicated is sent and received in a code operating in terms of symbols. It has been held therefore that the principles which have arisen in telephone engineering may be applicable to the problems of the handling of messages by the nervous system and thus to skill.

Broadbent[220] for instance states that 'a nervous system acts to some extent as a single communication channel, so that it is meaningful to regard it as having a limited capacity.' Thus it has already been pointed out that when two signals occur close together a person often takes a relatively long time to respond to the second signal. The information-capacity of the human motor-system in particular tasks has been determined.

Crossman[221] for example calculated the channel-capacity of subjects carrying out a pursuit tracking task. He postulated 'that the human sensori-motor apparatus comprises at least two functionally distinct parts. The first, which may be called the Decision or D-mechanism is concerned with translating visual or other signals into orders which the second, the Effector or E-mechanism, carries out'. These two mechanisms have different capacities and therefore a subject's performance at any task depends on 'exactly how the two mechanisms are loaded and on the time-relations between their activities and the external situation'. Fig. 14 shows Crossman's schematic representation of information-flow in the human perceptual-motor system.

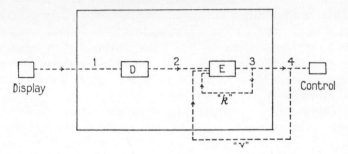

FIG. 14.

1. Visual signal; 2. Effector command; 3. Muscle action; 4. Hand movement. "*k*" Kinaesthetic feed-back path; "*v*" Visual feed-back path.

Information in the technical sense must be distinguished from signals or stimuli for the amount of information depends on the extent to which the signal is expected. Events which are not expected convey a great deal of information whereas variations in the environment which are predictable give very little information and those which are certain are redundant. Thus the beginner and the expert may face the same situation and be presented with the same display of signals. In the case of the beginner there are a very large number of unexpected stimuli presenting a large amount of information and since there is a limit to his information-capacity, he cannot handle it satisfactorily. Also he will increase the amount of information with which he is having to deal by the irregularity and unpredictability of his own responses. To the skilled performer on the other hand many of the signals are redundant for they are expected and therefore give no information. The expert only has to pay attention to a few important cues and so he has to deal with relatively little information. In this sense then the outstanding games player will be the person who has a large number of appropriate actions which deal with stimuli which have been experienced many times before and particularly who respond to the earliest signal in any connected sequence of signals, thus leaving time and information-capacity free to deal with unexpected signals.

One of the most important factors then in this type of skilled performance is the ability to select and pay attention to the right signals and to ignore irrelevant stimuli. Meredith[222] has said that 'the job of the instructor should not primarily be to persuade his pupil to make certain movements, but rather first to identify, and then to communicate the information which determines the control of these movements'.

The extent to which machine analogies and concepts developed in engineering throw light on the mechanisms involved in skill is open to argument. However new ideas do frequently lead to a stimulation of interest in a subject and sometimes to helpful deductions. Information theory for example has provided a fresh way of examining events within the nervous system and has drawn particular attention to the principles which govern the discarding of information. Anyone interested in skill should follow developments and abstract any useful deductions which may be made from experimental work in these fields.

# VIII

## THEORIES OF LEARNING

NOW THAT the acquisition of skill has been dealt with in some detail and the practical issues have been reviewed, it is necessary to turn to a more theoretical examination and consider how far the principles which have been elicited accord with various theories of learning as a whole.

In Chapter I learning was briefly discussed. The definition that 'learning is the internal neural process assumed to occur whenever a change in performance, not due to growth or fatigue, exhibits itself'[223] does not imply that the change is necessarily an improvement. Bad ways can be learned as well as good. Frequently a person who learns squash rackets without advice or good models builds up his strokes from the wrong basic position on the court. These poor techniques permit him to play a game but limit his progress. Many tennis players who were told to put the thumb across the racket for a backhand stroke interpreted this direction incorrectly and subsequently performed the stroke in such a way that little improvement with practice could be shown. Many good games players wishing to become better have learned new methods which have failed to improve their performances judged by end results. In any case it is not always easy to determine whether improvement has been made. Kuo[224] studied the behaviour of kittens towards mice. From his experiments it appears that the characteristic predatory behaviour is not instinctive and that gently nurtured kittens will live in peace and goodwill with mice sharing their quarters. Aggression in cats seems to be largely the result of training by their elders.

Who is to judge whether this learning is an improvement or not?

Learning, then, has much wider application than to skill alone. An increase in skill implies improvement but much that is learned is not skilful and may even prove detrimental to the learner. Learning is not co-extensive with skill but skill nevertheless is learned. In order therefore to understand the views of psychologists on skill it is advisable to consider briefly three of the many different viewpoints on learning.

First there is the theory which describes learning as the formation of conditioned responses. This is based on experimental work conducted by Pavlov.[225] When a dog is given food, saliva is produced. This is part of a reflex pattern of responses which may include not only secretion but also motor reactions in neck, jaw and legs. Pavlov found that he could train dogs so that the salivary response would be produced when a bell was sounded or when a light came on. He did this by first getting a dog used to the experimental conditions of being in a harness and so on. He then gave the dog the stimulus of (say) the bell to which he wished him to respond and immediately afterwards gave him the food. This was done many times with the time between the stimulus and the food gradually being increased. Ultimately the dog would produce saliva when the bell was rung even though there was no food. The dog had learned to respond to the bell. The conditioned stimulus of the bell had been substituted for the primary stimulus of the food and the dog made a conditioned response in place of the original reflex action. The conditioned response was not identical with this reflex for it did not necessarily include the same movements but salivation was of course common to both.

A conditioned response may not occur if the environment is slightly changed. Pavlov's pupils for instance often found that when they wished to demonstrate to him the conditioned response of one of their dogs, his presence caused the reflex not to work. Although the apparently important stimuli were present the dog did not react to these key sign stimuli but to the whole pattern of the environment and this had been changed by the addition of Pavlov.

Conditioning, when the term is used to mean the attaching of part of a reflex action to a new stimulus, is frequent up to the age of about three or four years. After that age, conditioning becomes less dependable though it is possible to demonstrate it experimentally in adults.

Some have suggested that the conditioned response is the prototype of all learning. As has already been pointed out (page 131) there are indeed a very large number of unlearned reflex responses which operate at spinal cord and sub-cortical levels. These innate responses can become conditioned to new stimuli and must form the basis for many movements. Learning however seems to involve more than conditioning as the term has been used here. For example if rats are trained to run through a maze to food and are then put in the same maze when it contains water they will swim through to their goal. If their brains have been damaged so that they cannot walk they will roll through the maze and will therefore still bring about the pre-determined end result. But in each case they are making what appears to be a completely new set of motor responses so one cannot say that this is straightforward conditioning. Instead the rats appear to have associated the stimuli with the 'path to the goal'.

Some psychologists have extended the use of the term conditioning to include not only elementary reflexes but also any 'complex of movements' which is in process at the time when the stimulus occurs.[226] Thus a combination of stimuli which have been accompanied by a movement will, on recurring, tend to be followed by that movement. There are many theories of learning based on the idea that stimulus and response become associated with one another. When a stimulus occurs the nerve impulse is believed to encounter a certain amount of resistance at the synapses and when this is broken down then a bond is formed between stimulus and response. Under what circumstances can this happen?

When a child is first given a bat and ball he learns by trial and error. Even where a person has been given a clear idea of his goal and the best way to attain it, he still usually proceeds in a way which is best described by the phrase, trial and error, although his efforts are by no means completely random. The essentials of trial and error behaviour have been stated by Woodworth[227] to be:

1. A 'set' to reach a certain goal.

2. Inability to see any clear way to the goal.
3. Exploring the situation.
4. Seeing or somehow finding leads, possible ways to reach the goal.
5. Trying these leads.
6. Backing off when blocked in one lead and trying another.
7. Finally finding a good lead and reaching the goal.

When a good movement or answer has been found then sometimes rapid learning is achieved and sometimes the goal has to be reached many times by chance before apparent progress is made. According to 'bond psychologists' certain conditions make the learning more likely and these have been formulated as laws. Two of these will now be mentioned. The first is the law of exercise which states that the more frequently a stimulus and response are associated with each other, the more likely that particular response is to follow the stimulus. This implies then that one learns by doing and that one cannot learn a skill, for instance, by watching others. It is necessary to practise because by doing so the bond between stimulus and response will be strengthened.

But when a complex skill is first tried many more wrong responses are made than right ones so there must be some other factor which will cause the bond with the better response to be the one which is strengthened. This factor is the feeling which accompanies each action. A glow of satisfaction when a correct movement has been made aids the stamping in of that movement whereas dissatisfaction helps to eradicate unfavourable actions. The law of effect therefore states that 'a modifiable bond' (between stimulus and response) 'is strengthened or weakened as satisfaction or annoyance attends its exercise'.[228] The feeling-tone should occur as close to the response as possible and particularly is this so in the case of young children.

This law has important implications. Sheer repetition unaccompanied by feeling is not likely to have much result. Thorndike[229] wrote that 'repetition of a connexion in the sense of the mere sequence of the two things in time has then very, very little power, perhaps none, as a cause of learning'. A teacher must then help to produce feelings of satisfaction in the pupil when a good movement has been achieved. People are more likely to repeat experiences which are a joy and are satisfying to them. The satisfaction results in reinforcement of the association between stimulus and response. The feeling of dissatisfaction should perhaps be used less often but sometimes a poor movement which has been done for some time feels right to the learner and the teacher must help the learner to eradicate the feeling of satisfaction which has become associated with it if improvement is desired.

Learning then depends on satisfactions and rewards. Individuals with poor techniques often fail to find satisfaction in a sport because only if there is a sound basis can progress continue and increasing pleasure be obtained from the activity. It is therefore important that the learner should get as nearly as possible to the right answer from the beginning. This is also true for another reason. An individual who has practised hard at a poor technique believing it to be satisfactory will have made the bond between stimulus and response a very strong one. He will have worn a nervous 'pathway' between stimulus and response which will be very difficult to change. When he tries to alter his techniques he will find his problem greater even than if he were learning for the first time. He usually has to remove the pleasurable feeling-tone and break down his own technique before he can build up anew and this makes him feel dissatisfied and unhappy. Unless he is quite convinced that his old methods are unsatisfactory for the attainment of the goal he has set himself he may become sceptical of the new methods, and prefer to go on with the old in spite of their obvious limitations. When he feels himself getting worse – and he must usually go through this stage if he is to break down old nervous 'pathways' – he may panic and decide to hang on to what he has. After all there is no certain guarantee that he will succeed in fixing the new 'pathways' in his nervous system. The decision to change will therefore usually depend on the amount of satisfaction he has with his present ability and this again is mainly a matter of the goal he wishes to achieve.

According to the theories based on the doctrine of association of stimulus and response, the following procedure in Guthrie's words must occur if an individual is to learn to produce a particular act in response to a particular stimulus or collection of stimuli.

'First the act must be somehow or other elicited or simply

awaited. If we know an effective stimulus for this, well and good. We must at least know that the act is within the animal's or the person's repertoire. We cannot teach cows to retrieve a stick because this is one of the things that cows do not do. It is because dogs' behaviour includes chasing sticks, taking objects into the mouth, walking and running, that we can build these into a conditioned response to a signal. At the beginning of the act we may speak a word or make a movement which will in time become the cue for the act.

'If we wish to teach a dog to come when he is called, one method will be to get him to come to us by hook or crook. There are no rules for this except what we know of dogs in general. We may hold up a bone, start running away from the dog, pull him towards us with a check line, or use any device which experience has suggested. While he is coming we speak the dog's name. If we take care not to speak the name on any occasion when we foresee that he will not come – when he is, for instance, chasing a cat or gnawing a bone (when we believe an unwanted response is dominant) – we can readily establish a stable conditioned response. We say that the dog "knows" his name. If we are so misguided as to try to call him back from the pursuit of a passing car before we have insured the effectiveness of calling, we have reconditioned the dog and made his name a signal for chasing cars, not for coming to us.'[230]

Three things may be noted from this. First that the individual must be capable of performing the act. He must be mature enough or strong enough or flexible enough. The movement must be a part of his repertoire. Secondly that the stage must be set so that the learner is likely to respond to the stimulus in the way which is desired. Thirdly that the stimulus should never be presented when the chances are that some other response will occur.

A habit may be considered as a path of preferred conduction between stimulus and response and associationists sometimes talk of 'wearing a pathway' in the nervous system. A habit is a learned stereotyped response which deals with the stimuli of the situation. It must not however be thought that the stimuli are each time exactly the same. In any situation there will be different stimuli present either in the external environment or internally or both. Suppose for instance that on the first occasion the individual responds to stimuli 1, 2, 3, . . . 100. When the situation next occurs stimuli 1–30 and 51–100 may be the same but 31–50 may be quite different. The response will therefore be different from the first response but nevertheless a fairly large part of it will be similar. The situation occurs again. Perhaps this time stimuli 1–25 and 30–100 are the same as on the first occasion but 26–29 are different and so on. Gradually the responses to stimuli which only occur occasionally will drop out and the learner will build up a stereotyped response to those stimuli which tend to recur. In time the habit may 'run itself off' as soon as a few of the initial stimuli are present. Guthrie has suggested that internal stimuli produced during the original series of responses now act as 'conditioners of the succession of movements'. Thus he says that 'the first acquisition of a new dance step consists in tentative movements which are directed by eye or the instructor's voice. On repetition, one movement becomes the substitute cue for the next and the series is partially independent of eye and voice'.[231]

But are habit and skill really one and the same? Clearly they are not, for a habit is a habit irrespective of its results but skill can only be defined in terms of the achievement of a previously specified or understood goal. Indeed a bad habit may prevent the acquisition of skill. According to the theory of association progress in skill is achieved by forming good habits and eliminating bad ones.

This may explain the building up of a skill like high jumping or diving but how far does it apply to games? In activities of this kind there cannot be one stereotyped series of movements for no two games are ever alike. It is doubtful if a person with a small number of good habits could be considered a good performer. A person who has 'grooved' his techniques too completely is often unable to adjust himself to differing conditions, for a small change in the external situation, if it is one which has not been experienced before, may interfere with the successful performance of a habit. Performers have often been upset by a games pitch in which the slope is unusual or by different equipment such as a peculiar ring to the basket in netball or basketball or by high altitudes where air resistance to the ball is less. Pear[232] pointed out that 'the slightest change in the external situation may interfere with the successful performance of a habit; a fraction of an ounce more or less on the head of a tennis racket . . . may interfere seriously with the smoothness of the game'.

The associationists therefore argue that to be a good games player thousands of habits fitted to different situations must be acquired and integrated. This does not seem too satisfactory an explanation of the footballer's or tennis player's skill for the number of habits required would be endless and the stamp of a good performer is that he can adjust 'on the spot'. This requires the ability to interfere with habits and, as has already been pointed out, this is a very difficult thing to do. A top-class tennis player is capable of 'scrambling' when necessary and producing strokes which would hardly be recognized as such by experts but which meet the need of the moment. Similarly, the opportunist at football is often one who can recognize the possibilities of a situation which he may never have seen before.

Habits and skills are certainly alike in some respects. They are both learned, and they both result in economy of effort and in actions which are not consciously controlled to any great extent. But the Cambridge school of psychologists has argued that there are marked differences. Oldfield[233] has stated that the 'differences as they appeared to Bartlett were broadly as follows: In the first place habit demands conformity to a prescribed standard sequence of motor acts while in skilled behaviour the same act is, strictly speaking, *never*, repeated. It may be that in some habitual acts, such as making the sign of the cross, the movement never becomes completely stereotyped. But in a skill the effectiveness of the behaviour is *dependent* upon the absence of stereotyping. At every instant the motor activity must be regulated by, and appropriate to, the external situation . . . what is learnt is not a series of individual acts . . . what we learn at tennis is not a set of strokes but how to *make* strokes appropriate to the moment. In a habit on the other hand, the more perfectly it is learnt the more the sequence of acts becomes independent of the environment, and the more the integration is internal, so that when the first phase is initiated the rest follow'.

It is important to notice here the phrase 'independent of the environment' for this is a fundamental difference between games and, say, shot-putting or diving or olympic gymnastics. The above description of a habit fits the latter activities quite well whereas the references to skill fit the former. But the physical educationist would call all these activities skills and certainly to excel in one or the other requires a similar amount of effort. But do they require the same sort of training?

Before this is discussed a third view of learning to which Bartlett and many others subscribe must be considered. This view which is based on field theory is fundamentally different to that of association theory. The latter considers that wholes are developed by combining parts and these parts can be dissociated again at will and recombined to form other wholes. Isolated reflexes can be combined into more complex actions and by trial and error experience, patterns of movement can be developed and connected with appropriate stimuli. Habits can be formed and skill built up. Field theory cannot accept this as a fruitful attitude to learning.

In the first place it is not agreed that the whole is the sum of its parts. Field theory holds that the organism has personality and reacts from the very beginning as a whole. As Koffka[234] puts it, other theories are based on the presupposition that 'single mental units called sensations are aroused in a simple manner by stimulation, and from them every other kind of experience is derived by a process of association'. This view 'that order comes only as a result of experience . . . that the consciousness of the newborn infant is nothing but a confused mass of separate sensations' is replaced by the assumption 'that a certain order dominates experience from the beginning'. In the first place then, attributes are implicitly understood to be parts of the nature of a thing and not as its whole nature so that the mind continues to look for further attributes. Parts may be differentiated but cannot be separated from the organization of the whole being. It may be possible to analyse a skill into parts after it has been acquired but the process of learning the skill has no close relationship to those parts. Instead the individual possesses a total response from the beginning and learns to narrow this down into precise partial patterns of movement which may be separated to various extents from the whole but never completely separated. The individual gains 'insight' and the greater the 'insight' the greater the skill.

In this connexion 'insight' learning is the opposite to trial and error. It involves a shift of attention so that the stimuli present are suddenly perceived in an entirely new way and in a way which leads one nearer to one's goal. Woodworth[235] has described an experiment in which a little girl of 40 months was placed in a play-pen. Inside the pen was a stick and outside there was another stick and a toy. In order to reach the toy the two sticks had to be joined together. For several days the child tried with one stick or the other and showed every sign of frustration. Then she suddenly had the right idea and obtained the toy. This abrupt change to mastery of the situation arises from a sudden appreciation of the relationships involved and is called insight learning. In many cases insight is dependent on past experience which has, of course, been full of trial and error but there do nevertheless seem to be instances of real insight which cannot be explained merely as a carry-over from previous situations. The author, when playing an exhibition tennis match against a girl who returned every ball 10 feet over the net to a good length so that it bounced into the stop-netting and was 6–0, 4–0 down, felt that she had an insight when she suddenly realised that she could win by standing in the middle of 'no-man's land' and drive-volleying every ball! She certainly solved a new problem by a new mode of behaviour. Similarly a good golfer will get out of a difficulty which he has never met before. Insights of this kind are not just transfers from previous situations but are a completely new organization of a whole system of experiences. This perception, according to field theory, is an indivisible whole.

The adjustments then which the organism makes increases its insight into the whole and permits the discovery of dynamic relationships. Kohler[236] presented apes and a child with two grey boxes, one brighter than the other. The brighter one contained food and the other was empty. When they had learned to choose the brighter box the less bright box was taken away and another box brighter than the remaining one was substituted. The apes chose the brightest box and not the one which had previously had food in it. The same thing happened in the experiment with the child.

The apes or child did not respond to the colour sensation but to the relation 'brighter than'. Kohler therefore concluded that responses are not made to sensations as such but to the pattern of the stimuli or configuration.

Two interesting quotations may make this viewpoint clearer: 'The logic of some dance-form such as the fox-trot is not a series of different steps. That logic centres on a certain rhythmic co-ordination, from which all the various steps radiate out'.[237] It is not then a matter of acquiring a series of operations one by one and stringing them together but of getting the central consideration clearer, of gaining insight into it. The more the insight, the greater the skill.

'In man the mastery of the necessary motor controls in swimming is like a delayed perceptual insight. . . . It is not enough . . . to breathe correctly, to hold the head and body in the right position, to kick properly and to swing the arms in the desired fashion, if all these things are done without reference one to the other. These things must all be assembled into a working unit before the skill of swimming as a configured action really exists.' 'It is always the total organism that does the learning and not just those outer mechanisms that are most conspicuously involved.'[238]

This means that transfer cannot, as is the view of the associationists, be due to identical elements but must take place because the individual acquires insight into the configuration. Learning then is a process of discovering and understanding relationships.

At this stage it is desirable to consider how these learning theories may contribute to an understanding of the acquisition of skills in physical education and physical recreation. Suppose a skill such as shot-putting is first considered. Here the best performer in theory will be the one who has the best style mechanically speaking, who can produce most power and who can perform this technique under any circumstances. Thus the best performers will tend to be those who can ignore the signals arising from the external environment. The learner will therefore spend his time first on building up a pattern of movement which is as close as possible to the theoretical best for his build and then on practising this pattern so that it will become virtually a habit. From then on any improvement will be made by increasing the strength and applied power of the performer. There may possibly be criticism of this view from shot-putters who might argue that a strong wind or a varying surface may have to be taken into account. Theoretically however these will affect the athletes in a similar way and in any case are of exceedingly small importance so far as this particular skill is concerned. Poulton[239] has called this type of skill a closed skill without external requirements. Next the skills of diving or vaulting may be considered. Here the external requirements may affect the skill but the effects are likely to be predictable to the skilled man. The skill can be thought of as the building up of a number of habits to meet predictable requirements or, as Poulton would say, these are closed skills with predictable requirements.

If however a skill such as association football is considered other factors become important. In this game an individual may have good patterns of movement but if he does not do the right action at the right moment he is almost useless as a player. Thus here it is the insight into the display which is of major importance. The need here as Bartlett[240] says is for the performer to be 'in touch with demands which come from the outside world' and thus the messages from the distance receptors and their interpretation become vital. It would seem necessary therefore for the learner in this case to pay more attention to perceptual learning and to understanding the important signals in the display. Poulton[241] would call this an open skill which he defines as 'a skill which has to fit either an unpredictable series of environmental requirements, or a very exacting series, whether predictable or unpredictable'.

Other complex skills may lie somewhere between shot-putting and association football in the relative importance of external to other factors. Swimming or running 100 yards would seem to be near to shot-putting in that if the necessary pattern of movements can be produced habitually on the sound of the starter's gun, winning or losing will depend on the relative merits in terms of the mechanical and physical advantages of the individual concerned.

In short-distance sprinting, in shot-putting and also in the case of some gymnastic skills the effectiveness of behaviour does seem to depend on stereotyping. The skill of running or swimming a long-distance race may involve tactical considerations and so perceptual aspects depending on distance receptors begin to have some importance though not so much as in team games where adaptability to the external environment must be of a high order.

The view is therefore put forward[242] that there is a continuum from skills which are predominantly habitual through to skills which are predominantly perceptual. At one end of the continuum are skills in which 'conformity to a prescribed standard sequence of motor acts' is all-important and at the other are skills in which 'at every instant the motor activity must be regulated by and appropriate to the external situation' and in which the correct interpretation of messages from the distance receptors is vital. In between lie skills at various places along the continuum depending on the relative importance in the perfected skill of habitual and perceptual aspects.

There is one point here which should be clarified. Being at one end or the other of the continuum has no implications affecting the difficulty of becoming an outstanding performer in that skill. To become expert in closed skills an individual must acquire well-timed muscular co-ordinations which are almost perfect and then work hard on building up strength, power and, in many cases, endurance and mobility. He cannot hide any deficiencies in skill or in his physical attributes whether innate or acquired. To become expert in open skills such as team and racket games, fencing and boxing, on the other hand, an individual must be capable of dealing with a great variety of situations but he can, if he is skilled, control these situations to a certain extent. He can therefore make up for deficiencies in his techniques and in his physical abilities. Maureen Connolly was able to become the best woman singles tennis player in the world when she had virtually no volley at all. In 1931 P. D. Howard captained the English rugby football team, having played throughout his career with the considerable physical disability of wastage in the leg. In open skills no one can ever have all the attributes and skills of a theoretically perfect performer.

One difficulty which is inherent in any discussion on highly complex skills is that a person has never attained perfection and thus skill is not static but is continually being changed in an attempt to better it. Nevertheless it would appear that in skills at the end of the continuum where the pattern of movement is by far the most important factor, it is vital for competitive purposes to have a more or less stereotyped series of actions. In shot-putting for instance it is the technique of the bodily skill which is of major importance and therefore in competition the nearer this is to a mechanically perfect habit the better. Another criticism may be that in fact the same end-result is not always achieved in exactly the same way and not even the same muscles are always used in an identical fashion. Nevertheless one would expect in theory that the perfect shot-putting technique by one individual would be carried out in a set way. Certainly this is the goal at which performers in athletics, swimming, diving, vaulting and compulsory figure-skating aim.

It may also be said however that some teachers concerned with games activities seem to have the same view and these may object to the idea that external requirements should affect the way in which the techniques are built up. Some coaches certainly appear to think that skill in, for instance, tennis is very largely determined by having a certain number of correct habits in the form of outstanding strokes rather than by being able to choose the best response at one's command to deal with and control the situation.

If the idea of a continuum is a valid one then it is important for the learner, teacher or coach to decide where the particular skill with which he is concerned lies in it for this will determine the relative importance which he must attach to the various factors and therefore the type of training which must be given. For instance if the problem of delaying the onset of fatigue is considered it may well be that the proportions of time to be spent on particular types of training should vary according to the place of the activity in the continuum. In recent years there have been great improvements in the measured performances of top-class swimmers and track and field athletes and these appear to have been caused mainly by very hard training programmes. The building up of strength and endurance has presumably, among other things, delayed the onset of fatigue. But there are different forms of fatigue. In fencing and in racket games, the environment, including the opponent's actions, is of vital importance. A large part of these skills involve judgement and the taking of decisions so that fatigue may be largely 'mental'. In running a mile on the other hand, although the opponent's efforts have to be taken into account this is a relatively minor factor. If an individual's mechanism is better than anyone elses and he can run faster then it is fundamentally a matter of making sure that the mechanism operates to full efficiency on the day.

Welford[243] has observed that 'changes in skill for better or worse may be located in many different mechanisms. Of these, however, the peripheral receptor and effector organs are probably of comparatively minor importance. Well-formed efficient sense organs and muscles will favour the establishment and maintenance of skill, and impairment of either will tend to cause its breakdown, but a great many experiments and clinical observations on both animals and human beings have shown that there can be impairments of both sense organs and peripheral effector organs with relatively little loss of skill.

'Much more important would seem to be the central receptor, translatory and effector mechanisms concerned with the organization of data and the shaping of action'.

This view does not seem so applicable to skills at the habitual end of the continuum but it would seem to have considerable validity where activities at the games end of the continuum are concerned.

The suggestion is therefore made that the fatigue encountered in swimming and running is mainly in the effector mechanism so that hard physical training can make a great difference to performance in the longer events. In fencing and the racket games on the other hand the receptor and translation mechanisms are as important as the effector. Many tennis players would acknowledge that they can play tennis all day provided they are a little more skilled than their opponents even though they take a great deal of physical exercise in the process. If they are able to dictate the game they do not have to act under mental pressure and to a large extent have plenty of time to execute their techniques. When however their opponents are as good or a little better than they are then for large parts of the time the task is paced in the sense that the important signals and the time limits for action are outside their control. But any individual is limited in his capacity to notice the appropriate signals, to transfer information and to retain short-term impressions and when he is fatigued it appears that this capacity is further reduced. Those stimuli which occur infrequently but are nevertheless important tend to be ignored. The onlooker may note that the tired player is reacting slowly or on occasions is not reacting at all and that many of his movements seem unnecessary and not appropriate to his task. The performer himself often becomes obsessed with some particular difficulty or with his own discomforts. But the way the performer looks or feels may not be a true guide to what is wrong. The breakdown in skill may not arise from fatigue or lack of fitness in the muscular or cardio-vascular systems but may arise from the limitations of the central mechanisms.

In an experiment by Singleton[244] it was shown that the deterioration of performance, which in this particular case appeared to be localized almost entirely in the central mechanisms, increased with the perceptual difficulty of the task. This means that in skills where interpretation of the situation is important, time in training should be spent on simplifying and clarifying the cues for action. In order then for an individual not to suffer mental fatigue it is necessary for him to spend a great deal of time and effort on improving his skill so that he need no longer be subject to the kind of pressures which cause it.

In lawn tennis 'an improvement in performance obtained by strengthening and speeding-up exercises which concentrate on the effector mechanism is likely to be of diminishing value as the limits of performance are approached. There is even some ground for believing that over-concentration on the effector side might lower the optimal level of performance'.[245] The general view that top performances in lawn tennis are less skilful than they used to be even though performances in athletics and swimming have greatly improved may therefore well be true. In team games, too, attention should be given to the mental aspects of the activity for the more skilled the players are the less the physical effort they are likely to have to make. The fact that Stanley Matthews is able to maintain a position in a League football team at the age of forty-six is, in this light, an understandable feat.

The position then which a skill occupies in the continuum

can have many implications in terms of training. Athletic, gymnastic, swimming and diving skills require the spending of a great deal of time and effort on habit formation; and on strengthening and power-building exercises. The skilled performer gradually acquires a mental 'model' of the movement pattern and the ability to sense immediately any departure from it. He learns to make adjustments either at the time or in the next performance of the pattern of movements and so bring the action back into line with the model. He must continually reduce the range of variation.

In games and other open skills on the other hand a great deal of attention must be paid to the signals from the external environment, to the judgements which must be made and to the building up of appropriate but varied responses. The games player must not always react to the same situation in the same way. The skilled performer must therefore have knowledge of the tools or techniques at his command and use them to suit the situation. The greater the range of movements the better, provided they are under sufficient control to be produced appropriately, but some very good performers possess a relatively small number of techniques. The outstanding games player seems to react to situations much sooner than the average performer. This is probably due in part to his identification of cues which appear early rather than having to wait for the later and more obvious ones.

Much more knowledge is needed of the signals in any particular game to which skilled players react. Very little work has been done on identifying the important cues and this seems a rich field for the extension of skill teaching in the future.

The decision as to where a skill lies in the continuum will often be a difficult one to make and may not be determinable once and for all time. Thus the position of lawn tennis appears to have changed. The perceptual factors which were of great importance seem to be of less significance in the men's game on grass now that the service has become such a dominating influence. By having several services which are mechanically outstanding and which can be produced habitually, an individual can under present conditions on fast courts so dictate the play when he is serving that the possible responses of the opponent are reduced to a small number with which the server can learn to deal in a number of set ways. Under these circumstances the patterns of movement and particularly those for the service may become more important than the signals from the external environment.

The view put forward in this chapter suggests that association and conditioning theories may be more helpful in considering athletic, swimming, skating and recognized gymnastic skills whereas field theory is essential to the understanding of games.

# IX

## CRITERIA OF SKILL

SKILL HAS FREQUENTLY been discussed in terms of standards by which it may be judged. Pear[246] for example considered skill to be an integration and organization of bodily habits and one of the aspects of habit which he selected as relevant was that 'these movements are performed with less effort and less attention than are non-habitual movements'. Guthrie[247] has suggested that skill is the reduction of a response to its essential movements only. 'The activity is limited to the muscles and the movements required for the performance. This process, of course, is never complete. Perfect grace, which means the use of only the essential muscles and this use only to the point necessary for the action, is only approximated, never reached.'

In the case of these and many other writers a criterion of skill is the degree of muscular co-ordination which is attained in the act. Attention is paid mainly to the motor aspects of skill and to the qualities of the movements made. It is true that smoothness of movement and grace are frequently characteristic of skill but judgement of the relative skill of two performers cannot be made on this basis alone except where grace is the sole criterion of success. In many activities there are occasions when a jerky movement to deal with a variable would be a sign of skill because skill would be measured by performance.

Other writers have accentuated the perceptual aspect of skill. Crossman[248] referring to manual work has gone so far as to write that 'in the course of acquiring skill, perceptual structure of a worker's performance will be found to alter much more than his actual movements and it is this alteration and improvement in perceptual organization which really constitutes skill'. Meredith[249] has said that skill is 'always a carefully graded response to a task subject to endless subtle variations' and Welford[250] observes that 'perhaps the most conclusive point that one can make about skill or skills is that they do not depend on fixed patterns of movement or fixed methods of thinking but are concerned with the flexible fitting of means to ends'.

Many psychologists then and particularly those interested in industrial skills have stressed the importance of the receptor and translation mechanisms in the learning of physical skills. At Cambridge a great deal of experimental work has been concerned with patterns of stimuli and with skills in which the display of signals from the external environment is of vital importance to performance. The stimuli which are perceived are however internal as well as external and therefore include kinaesthetic sensations. According to Gooddy[251] an individual can only learn the sensations which accompany a movement and therefore patterns of sensation are learned, not patterns of movement. The suggestion is that since skilled movements tend to break down when they are consciously thought about, the learner should be spending his time rather on increasing his understanding of the needs of a situation by more specific and more precise interpretation of the sense impressions he receives. Hellebrandt[252] writes that 'perhaps the acuity we should strive for is not enhanced general body awareness but rather a more sharply defined and specific sensitivity to what is happening in those key manoeuvres upon which the success or failure of a complex movement pattern may depend'.

In teaching skills in physical education the stress has tended to be on general body awareness and on the muscular coordination of the effector processes. Certainly the overt motor act is the most obvious part of a skill to an onlooker.

But skill is also affected by the amount of insight which in turn depends on what the individual perceives. At any time there are a very large number of stimuli present both outside and inside the individual. An individual cannot perceive them all and so he selects those which he considers important and groups them so that they make sense to him. The stimuli arrive through many different sensory channels which may change in importance as learning proceeds. The stimuli from the visual, auditory, tactile, kinaesthetic and other sense organs are all organized to form a perceived whole. Frequently there are gaps in the actually observed stimuli and these he fills up on the basis of what he has experienced before. The footballer may move into a space at the appropriate moment. Two hockey players may look the same when hitting for goal, but the goal-keeper may react differently through previous knowledge of them. The tennis player on first playing squash may try to follow the ball through the wall.

The unskilled performer may notice a number of stimuli but he will be unable to perceive which are the important ones or what the responses should be. He will tend not to perceive any pattern to the stimuli and since the capacity to take in information is limited the number of stimuli to which he can pay attention will be relatively few. The skilled person on the other hand possesses a mental framework which takes into account a large number of the stimuli which have occurred before. He notices small changes from the expected display and is therefore able to react to them quickly.

The experienced tennis player will notice that his opponent is left-handed during the preliminary practice before a match and can therefore arrange his tactics accordingly. The unskilled may play the whole match without realizing this fact. Again the skilled tennis player after he has been playing an opponent for a short time will know in many cases the type of service and the general direction of the ball before the server actually contacts the ball. The beginner will not know until the ball has arrived. The expert diver will notice any small difference in the spring-board and be able to adjust it to his liking (where there is equipment for so doing). The skilled rugby footballer will adjust his kicks according to the wind. These examples show that there are two stages where open skills are concerned. First, the skilled man perceives the change in the pattern of stimuli and secondly he takes appropriate action to meet the change.

Frequently in order to take appropriate action he has not only to notice that there is a change but also he has to estimate the rate of change. For example, when bringing a dinghy alongside a buoy the helmsman must make continuous adjustments based not only on the error but on the rate at which it is diminishing. The good ball player must also be able to estimate accurately rates of change.

Prior experience greatly affects how and what is perceived because individuals are continually trying to fit new information into some general framework. This framework which is usually based on previous experience is both spatial and temporal. When a game is being played the other players and the ball are perceived as located in space and their positions are related to the lines of the field and to each other. The events which occur are also noted as being related in time, and series of events can be appreciated as forming sequences or rhythms. It is on the basis of such a framework that anticipation of future events can be made. Timing and anticipation have been put forward then as criteria of skill.

According to Conrad[253] 'timing in its ordinary everyday sense refers to the temporal "lay-out" of a series of responses'. But confusion can arise in that temporal lay-out may refer to the way in which the movements of the body fit into each other or it may refer to the time factor in the whole activity both in a short-and a long-term sense.

In javelin-throwing, for instance, timing refers to the duration of the constituent actions in a pattern of movement. A javelin-thrower with good timing so orders the duration of the constituent actions in the throw that maximal force is produced at the appropriate moment. The muscle fibres required for the action respond in such a way as to produce maximum force at the best moment to result in maximum effect. In this case, then, good timing is only attained when the technique is in accord with the mechanical requirements of the skill as related to each individual's body. Similarly in skills such as high- and long-jumping, shot-putting and discus-throwing and also in sprinting or hurdling short distances. So far as these types of skill are concerned any smoothness results from the fact that mechanical efficiency is greater when movements flow into one another and no excess muscular contractions are executed.

If however the movements have to be performed over such a period of time that decisions on pacing have to be made then timing may refer to the ordering of a series of responses so that the best results in the long run may be secured. Thus in a long-distance swimming race good timing does not refer so much to the technique of the winner but to his ability to arrange his efforts over the distance to the best advantage. Here he has to respond to a certain extent to the actions of his opponents and so external stimuli are of some importance.

There is a further complication in many activities such as racket games, fencing, judo and boxing in that 'the subject himself partly determines the temporal conditions in which the next response will have to be made'.[254] This partial control not only arises from the techniques used but also to a large extent from the ability to perceive and attend to the important changes in the display. Timing in these circumstances can be defined as 'creating the most favourable temporal conditions for response. Conditions for response are considered to be favourable when the response can be made with the least hurry, at the best moment, whilst leaving the organism in a satisfactory post-response state'. 'Bad timing in the present makes timing in the immediate future more difficult' whereas 'good timing in fact provides the optimum temporal conditions for response'.

In cases of this kind good timing is not directly observed but it is inferred from the fact that the performer is able to make unhurried and smooth movements. The good tennis player seems to have all the time in the world to make his strokes and do what he wishes with the ball. Good timing so far as the performer is concerned normally results in a pleasant feeling of ease and lack of effort relative to the results achieved.

Bartlett[255] has pointed out that 'there are limits, upper and lower, within which the timing can rapidly fluctuate and the essential adaptive spacing of actions still be maintained. Outside those limits only the skill breaks down'. Thus the tennis player can keep his timing even, on occasions, when losing. But if the pressure becomes too great, the person has not time to pay attention to the important signals in the display. This results in his having less time in which to act and so, at a certain point, his technique breaks down and any feeling of good timing is lost. The same type of thing can also happen to a whole team in football or hockey. Pressure can be produced not only by the speed of the ball but also by the unexpectedness of the situation. Frequently movement takes less time than deciding on the action and so, if the ball is put by the opponent in an unexpected place, the response is slowed down because of the need to make a sudden decision and pressure is increased. Anticipation, the ability to look forward and judge correctly what is going to happen next, is therefore an aid to good timing in many circumstances. The person who can anticipate well can start to respond early to a situation which is arising and he therefore truly has more time in which to make the necessary movements.

Anticipation may occur in at least two ways. When a footballer kicks a ball in the air its path is determined at the moment of impact. The unskilled performer may have to wait until the ball has almost landed before he acts. The skilled man on the other hand will estimate the future position of the ball on the basis of a small number of signals occurring very early on. Similarly in cricket, the path of the ball is determined when it leaves the bowler's hand and, if the wicket can be relied on, the batsman can begin to prepare his stroke on the basis of signals arising from the bowler's action and on his knowledge of the bowler's abilities. In these cases then anticipation is based on the ability to predict future events from the first few signals in an invariant sequence.[256]

It is difficult for people to learn to anticipate in this way where conditions are bad. For instance if cricket is practised on bad surfaces the batsman will not be dealing with an invariant sequence until after the ball has hit the ground and will therefore not learn to pay due attention to the bowler's behaviour. The tennis player who learns on poor courts will build up techniques which stand him in good stead in his local club but which prove of little use in the championships of the world. Poor conditions are notoriously great levellers of performance too, for the skilled performer can no longer use his superior anticipatory abilities to advantage and indeed they may even prove disadvantageous. For example a good tennis player knows how balls with top-spin react and therefore adjusts his movements accordingly when his opponent uses it. But on a bad surface any bound may result and therefore the expert's response may be worse than that of the individual who normally waits to see what the ball will do before responding. This then is merely repeating what has previously been stated, that an activity should be learned and practised in the conditions in which it is to be used. If it is desired that standards should be high then conditions must be good, otherwise anticipation will not be learned.

Anticipation may also occur where an invariant sequence is not involved. The skilled games player has to anticipate the actions of his opponents and of his team-mates. In this case his prediction cannot be certain but must be based on the probability of certain events occurring. He has to be able to weigh up the odds. He is more likely to be accurate in his prediction than the unskilled because he has learned the relative significance of various signals and therefore knows the ones to which he should pay attention. Decision-making is of major importance. Some games players never seem to be able to do the right thing at the right moment whereas others seem to have developed the ability of keeping some unorthodox move up their sleeve and producing it when the occasion demands it. One might perhaps cite Ken Scotland in rugby football and Allan Jay in fencing as people with this ability. Could not games ability of this type be developed to a certain extent by the method of teaching? It is true in games that the unorthodox or disguised action at the appropriate moment is so valuable that it may on occasions be worth sacrificing technical perfection for it. Games and other activities such as fencing in which the opponent's actions directly affect one's own and vice versa, should be predominantly a battle of wits and this aspect should be learned by children in their later years at school.

From the above discussion it can be seen that there are different kinds of timing and that smoothness of movement and good anticipation are frequent aspects of skill but may not always be present. The criteria which apply to any particular skill and the importance therefore of different aspects of training are determined in part by the position of that skill in the continuum.

Bartlett[257] has suggested that 'the best single measure of skill is one of its "range of constancy", its degree of resistance to disintegrating conditions', and Lewis[258] related consistency in performance to skill in driving a motor-car. But even if it were shown that an aspect of skilled performance is its consistency it does not follow that a consistent performance is necessarily skilled. A golfer who invariably 'slices' or a javelin thrower who always hesitates for a fraction of time after the run and before executing the throw may be very consistent but would not be considered skilful.

None of these criteria can therefore be used as a standard by which all skill may be judged and they are therefore unsuitable for use in definitions of skill. It is partly for this reason and partly because it seems desirable to stress the specific nature of skill that the definition of skill as the learned ability to bring about pre-determined results with maximum certainty, often with the minimum outlay of time or energy or both, seems at the moment to be the most satisfactory one.

# X

## THE PLACE OF SKILL TRAINING
## IN PHYSICAL EDUCATION

SKILL IS SPECIFIC and so one may justifiably ask how much time should be spent on it in any programme of general physical education. The acquisition of skill is only one of many aims of such a programme in a school but it is one which continues to be important. Indeed it might well be argued that, because of social changes, a greater amount of time should be spent in the future on acquiring physical skills.

In the course of this book it has become clear first that the contribution of skill to performance varies between skills and secondly that the nature of skill itself varies from activity to activity. In order then that every child shall be able to find the area which appeals to him and in which he may experience success, a wide variety of activities must be presented. This does not mean simply a large number of physical skills but also skills from one end of the continuum to the other. In this way the opportunity is given for each child's particular capacities to show to advantage.

The teaching and training must be appropriate to the type of skill involved. When a skill is to be acquired it is first necessary to decide on the relative importance of skill, as defined in this book, when compared to all those other factors such as strength, flexibility, size and innate characteristics, which contribute to a skilled performance in the particular activity. This decision will influence the proportion of the total time available for spending on the activity which should be spent on skill.

Then the hours spent on acquiring skill must be used to the best advantage. The factors affecting the acquisition of skill which were discussed in Chapters III and IV must therefore be considered in relation to the position of the skill in the continuum and to its specific nature.

Much more research, preferably on a long-term basis, is required into the methods of teaching particular skills. More tests are needed to enable knowledge of results to be obtained speedily by the learner. More general information on the merits of different types of instruction and particularly on the use of mechanical analysis and of film is necessary and detailed knowledge of the cues to which skilled players react in those activities where the display is important would be invaluable.

Nevertheless factual information is not enough. The acquisition of skill is a function of man as a whole human being. Therefore all decisions on methods of acquisition must be adjusted to meet the particular requirements of each individual. The application of knowledge concerning skill to any individual acquiring a skill is still an art.

The aims of physical education must be modified as new facts are discovered and as conditions in society change, for the principles on which such aims are based must be in touch with the needs of society. Society today is changing its nature at a rapid rate. For example social conditions have altered so that many more people have a great deal of time and money available for spending on leisure activities. This is particularly true of the young workers under 25 years of age who now have something like £17 million a week to dispose of at their own discretion.[259] During the period from April 1956 to 1961 the hourly earnings of boys and girls in industry have risen by a bigger percentage than those of men, and girls are now earning nearly six times as much in an hour as they were earning before the war. By 1969 it is expected that the age group 15–24 will have increased in numbers by 1,300,000. A large proportion of those who now have a substantial amount of leisure and money to spend on it, have no traditions of leisure and are in the process of finding out how to use their free time. Their choice is greatly affected by their experiences as children.

Thus Nash[260] reports a study on the hobby interests of adults which found that the early years were the crucial ones. 'Some 78 per cent of all the hobby interests were laid down before the age of 12, over 62 per cent before the age of 10 and many before the age of 6.' Cauter and Downham[261] carried out a survey in Derby in 1953 and found that 39 per cent of the working class with a secondary or further education played games, compared with an equivalent figure of 49 per cent for the middle class and a figure of only 14 per cent for members of the working class with an elementary education. Economic factors could not be held responsible for these differences because the differences between the two classes when it came to watching sport were very small. The authors concluded that 'people with a similar education are much more likely to resemble one another in sporting habits, irrespective of class than they are to resemble people of their own class with a different education'. Surveys carried out between 1956 and 1958 for the Central Advisory Council for Education[262] (England) throw further light on the influence of the type of school and the parental occupation on the leisure-time activities of young people. Some of the information they collected is given in Tables 11 and 12.

If, therefore, the way people spend their leisure is considered to be important the schools must take this into account in their curriculum. The opinion has been expressed that education should not be so much for work as for leisure. Certainly if people are to recreate themselves in their leisure time they must have interests that use those faculties which nowadays are rarely needed at work, for the day of the craftsman in industry is over. McCloy[263] believes 'that any worthwhile activity executed skilfully enough to give the doer exquisite sensory pleasure is cultural'. But he goes on to point out that 'such pleasure is seldom achieved without skilled performances in which the satisfactions greatly outweigh the annoyances'.

The view that a certain amount of success, not necessarily at a high level, is necessary for people to continue to find an activity satisfying, has been put forward many times. As an example a survey[264] carried out in an industrial town in Finland in 1956 may be quoted. This survey found that active participation of men over twenty-one was dependent on how successful they had been in competition earlier on in their lives. The successful ones were more active than the unsuccessful.

TABLE 11

| Type of Activity in Clubs to which School-Leavers belonged at time of Interview | Boys who had left | | Girls who had left | |
|---|---|---|---|---|
| | Grammar or Technical Schools | Modern or All-age Schools | Grammar or Technical Schools | Modern or All-age Schools |
| | % | % | % | % |
| General youth club activity | 49 | 37 | 36 | 21 |
| Outdoor sports (inc. spectators clubs), walking, cycling | 37 | 18 | 19 | 4 |
| Indoor games | 16 | 9 | 7 | 3 |
| Scouts/Cadets/RedCross/other uniformed organizations | 11 | 6 | 7 | 4 |
| Arts/music/drama/debating | 22 | 3 | 17 | 3 |
| Hobbies/crafts/politics/ religions, etc. | 10 | 2 | 10 | 4 |
| Dancing only | 11 | 6 | 10 | 11 |
| Not members of any club | 21 | 44 | 40 | 65 |
| Number of School-Leavers = 100% | 561 | 878 | 520 | 801 |

Success, however, does not have to be assessed merely in terms of winning. Winning at all costs is an unsatisfactory aim. It is better to aim at the development of skill so that the individual becomes interested in the skill itself. Winning then merely sets the stamp on that skill by letting the performer know how much he has achieved. But this sort of attitude – the love for its own sake of skill in whatever medium it may be expressed – is best developed before adulthood.

Hodgkin[265] has asked whether skills are valued enough. He points out that 'more and more people turn, when they can, from the dull routines of town to seek the joyous hardships and dangers of rock, snow, speed and sea' and that 'many accidents stem from personal failure in men of moderate skill who should and could avoid them. The crux of the problem is neither caution nor rescue but skill'. He argues that 'pride in the craft, not pride in the achievement, should always be encouraged in the young climber' and contends that 'if we cherished skill more wisely we might court danger less'.

## TABLE 12

NATIONAL SERVICE MEN WHO LEFT SCHOOL AT 15 OR 16 WHO HAD PLAYED GAMES ACTIVELY DURING THE FIRST 3 YEARS AFTER LEAVING SCHOOL, IN RELATION TO PARENTAL OCCUPATION, SCHOOL AND MEMBERSHIP OF YOUTH ORGANIZATIONS.

| Active Games during first 3 years after leaving School | Whole Sampled Population | Parental Occupation | | | | Type of School | | Membership of Youth Organization | |
|---|---|---|---|---|---|---|---|---|---|
| | | Professional and other Non-manual | Skilled Manual | Semi-Unskilled Manual | Others | Selective | Non-selective | Active Membership | Not in Active Membership |
| Played Games | % | % | % | % | % | % | % | % | % |
| During all 3 years | 36 | 46 | 37 | 31 | 31 | 49 | 33 | 58 | 25 |
| During 1 or 2 years | 6 | 6 | 6 | 6 | 6 | 7 | 6 | 7 | 5 |
| Total | 42 | 52 | 43 | 37 | 37 | 56 | 39 | 65 | 30 |
| No active Games, etc. | 58 | 48 | 57 | 63 | 63 | 44 | 61 | 35 | 70 |
| Total | 6478 | 1002 | 3203 | 1685 | 588 | 1086 | 5392 | 2223 | 4255 |

A true appreciation of skill can best be built up in the earlier years through skills which are interesting to the children at their particular developmental level. Growth must be taken into account so that the acquisition of skill by children should not be based on adult needs and interests except in the later years. 'Adult' attitudes are, however, creeping back into the schools and this is partly because children now continue their education for a longer period and partly because of the continuing trend to mature at an earlier age. Tanner[266] writes that 'the present-day fourteen-year-old is, in physique and very probably in brain maturity also, the fifteen-year-old of a generation ago, and he must be treated accordingly'. Equipment, techniques and activities suitable for the last generation's children of fourteen will not be suitable for the fourteen-year-olds of today.

School, in terms of adult activities, is therefore of increasing importance and certainly the school-leaver ought to have acquired skill in one or two activities at a level high enough to encourage him to continue with them. But more important is the building up of an appreciation of skill in the younger person and the confidence that he can acquire skill in some quite new activity if he tries hard enough. The Finnish survey[267] already mentioned found that activity is cumulative. 'Active participation in one form is connected with active participation in another, and similarly passivity too is cumulative. The effect of successful competition is thus not limited to active participation in competitive sports but is connected with active participation in recreational sports, in spectator sports and with membership in sports clubs.' This means then that every child must acquire skill in an activity suitable to his age to a level where 'the satisfactions outweigh the annoyances'.

Most of the argument so far could and does refer to any form of skill and not necessarily to the gross motor skills. But the latter have particular appeal to children in their formative years and so they make a good area in which to teach an appreciation of skill. Many young people too express themselves most readily through practical media. But apart from these considerations physical recreation involving the gross motor skills is becoming more important because of another fundamental change in society. The amount of physical effort which any individual expends at work, in the home or in moving from place to place is continuously decreasing. Modern life relieves muscles at the expense of nerves. It is however generally conceded that some physical exercise is good for man and the Americans have recently been very disturbed about the health of their nation so far as basic physical fitness is concerned. Since England appears to be following in many ways in American footsteps such worries may soon be prevalent in English society also. But basic physical fitness depends upon a minimum of exercise and, apart from a few individuals who take exercise whether they like it or not because they believe it to be good for them, most people only engage in physical activity if they enjoy it. This enjoyment implies a level of skill sufficient to give satisfaction to the performer.

It may then be concluded that the needs for physical exercise and the joyful expression of skill are unlikely to be satisfied by most people in the course of their daily work and that use of some of their leisure time in physical activity is becoming increasingly necessary for the development of the whole personality. Physical recreation therefore has an important part to play but, in general, adults will only engage in some physical activity if they either have some skill on which to build or, because of previous success, are confident they can acquire it. Every individual therefore, by the time he leaves school, ought to have acquired enough skill in one or two activities to encourage him to continue with a skilled activity as an adult. It is vitally important that everyone shall fully comprehend the delight which skill can give for it is intrinsic motivation of this kind which will ensure that an individual takes part in some skilled activity all his life.

# REFERENCES

## MAIN REFERENCE BOOKS

*Psychology*, by R. S. Woodworth. Methuen and Co. Ltd. London.

*41st Yearbook of the National Society for the Study of Education.*
Part II. *The Psychology of Learning*, The University of Chicago Press,
Chicago. 1942.

*The Psychology of Learning*, by E. R. Guthrie. Harper & Brothers, New
York 1952.

*Manual of Child Psychology*, edited by L. Carmichael. Chapman and Hall
Ltd. London 1954.

*Handbook of Experimental Psychology*, edited by S. S. Stevens.
Chapman & Hall, London 1951.

*Ageing and Human Skill*, by A. T. Welford, O.U.P. London 1958.

*Research Quarterlies* published by the American Association for Health,
Physical Education and Recreation.

## KEY TO ABBREVIATION OF PERIODICALS

| | |
|---|---|
| Amer, J.P. | *American Journal of Psychology* |
| A.P.U. | *Applied Psychology Unit, Cambridge* |
| B.J.P. | *British Journal of Psychology* |
| B.M.J. | *British Medical Journal* |
| E.R. | *Educational Review* |
| J.Appl.P. | *Journal of Applied Psychology* |
| J.Ed.P. | *Journal of Educational Psychology* |
| J.Exp.P. | *Journal of Experimental Psychology* |
| J.Gen.P. | *Journal of General Psychology* |
| J.Genet.P. | *Pedagogical Seminary and Journal of Genetic Psychology* |
| J. of P.E. | *Journal of Physical Education* |
| O.P. | *Occupational Psychology* |
| P.B. | *Psychological Bulletin* |
| P.M. | *Psychological Monographs* |
| P.R. | *Psychological Review* |
| Q.J. exp.P. | *Quarterly Journal of Experimental Psychology* |
| R.Q. | *Research Quarterly* |

173

## References

CHAPTER I

¹ 'The psychology of skill.' B.M.J. No. 4511, June 1947, p. 890.
² Guthrie, E. R. *The Psychology of Learning*. Harper and Brothers, New York 1952, p. 136.
³ Gagné, R. M. and Fleishman, E. A. *Psychology and Human Performance*. Henry Holt and Company, New York 1959.

CHAPTER II

⁴ Krueger, W. C. F. 'Influence of difficulty of perceptual-motor task upon acceleration.' J.Ed.P. Vol. 38, p. 51.
⁵ Woodworth, R. S. *Psychology*. Methuen and Co. Ltd. London 1937, p. 246–footnote.
⁶ Kitson, H. D. *How to use your mind*. J. B. Lippincott and Co., London 1916, p. 158.
⁷ Bryan, W. L. and Harter, N. 'Studies in the physiology and psychology of the telegraphic language.' P. R. Vol. 4, 1897, p. 27–53.
⁸ Smith, M. Drury. 'Periods of arrested progress in the acquisition of skill.' B.J.P. (Gen.) Vol. 21, 1930, p. 1–28.
⁹ See reference 8.
¹⁰ See reference 7.
¹¹ See reference 7.
¹² See reference 8.

CHAPTER III

¹³ Cox, J. W. 'Some experiments on formal training in the acquisition of skill.' B.J.P. Vol. 24, 1933, p. 67–87.
¹⁴ Myers, C. S. Paper on 'Educability' given to the British Association 1928 – as reported by Cox – see reference 13, p. 68.
¹⁵ Davies, D. R. 'The effect of tuition upon the process of learning a complex motor skill.' J.Ed.P. 36, 1945, p. 352–65.
¹⁶ Welford, A. T. *Ageing and Human Skill*. Oxford University Press. London 1958, p. 27.
¹⁷ Judd, C. H. 'The relation of special training to general intelligence.' E.R. Vol. 36, 1908, p. 28–42.
¹⁸ See reference 13.
¹⁹ See reference 15.
²⁰ Gilbreth, F. B. and L. M. *Applied Motion Study*, Macmillan, New York 1919.
²¹ Ragsdale, C. E. 49th Yearbook of the National Society for the Study of Education. Part I, *Learning and Instruction*. P. 83. University of Chicago Press, Chicago 1950.
²² Kretchmar, R. T. Sherman, H. and Mooney, R. 'A survey of research in the teaching of sports.' R.Q. Vol. 20, 1949, pp. 238–49.
²³ Phillips, M. and Summers, D. 'Relation of kinesthetic perception to motor learning.' R.Q. Vol. 25, 1954, pp. 456–69.
²⁴ Anderson, T. 'A study of the use of visual aids in basket shooting.' R.Q. Vol. 13, 1942, pp. 532–7.

# References

[25] See reference 21.

[26] Priebe, R. E. and Burton, W. H. As reported by Meer, A. W. Vander in 'The economy of time in industrial training. An experimental study of the use of sound films in the training of engine lathe operators.' J.Ed.P. Vol. 36, 1945, pp. 65-90.

[27] Lockhart, A. 'The value of the motion picture as an instructional device in learning a motor skill.' R.Q. Vol. 15, 1944, pp. 181-7.

[28] Brown, H. S. and Messersmith, L. 'An experiment in teaching tumbling with and without motion pictures.' R.Q. Vol. 19, 1948, pp. 304-7.

[29] Nelson, D. O. 'Effect of slow motion loop films on the learning of golf.' R.Q. Vol. 29, 1958, pp. 37-45.

[30] Kinnear, A. D. 'Making swimming a pleasure.' Sport and Recreation. Vol. 1, No. 4, 1960, pp. 14-17.

[31] Battig, W. F. 'Transfer from verbal pre-training to motor performance as a function of motor task complexity.' J.Exp.P. Vol. 5, No. 6, 1956, pp. 371-8.

[32] Renshaw, S. and Postle, D. K. 'Pursuit learning under three types of instruction.' J.Gen.P. Vol. 1, 1928, pp. 360-7.

[33] Goodenough, F. L. and Brian, C. R. 'Certain factors underlying the acquisition of motor skill by pre-school children.' J.Exp.P. Vol. 12, 1929, pp. 127-55.

[34] See reference 13.

[35] See reference 17.

[36] Hendrickson, G. and Schroeder, W. H. 'Transfer of training in learning to hit a submerged target.' J.Ed. P. Vol. 32, 1941, pp. 205-13.

[37] See reference 17.

[38] Colville, F. M. 'The learning of motor skills as influenced by knowledge of mechanical principles.' J.Ed.P. Vol. 48, 1957, pp. 321-7.

[39] See reference 17.

[40] Whilden, P. P. 'Comparison of two methods of teaching beginning basketball.' R.Q. Vol. 27, 1956, pp. 235-42.

[41] Bartlett, F. C. Psychology and the Soldier. Cambridge University Press, London 1927.

[42] Bugelski, B. R. The Psychology of Learning. Methuen and Co. Ltd. London, 1956, p. 457.

[43] Lindsley, D. B. As reported by D. Wolfle in 'Training', Chap. 34, of Handbook of Experimental Psychology edited by S. S. Stevens. Chapman and Hall Ltd. London 1951, p. 1268.

[44] Trowbridge, M. H. and Cason, H. 'An experimental study of Thorndike's theory of learning.' J.Gen.P. Vol. 7, 1932, pp. 245-58.

[45] See reference 2. Pp. 146-7.

[46] Scott, M. G. and French, E. Evaluation in Physical Education. C. V. Mosby Company, St. Louis 1950, pp. 88-98.

[47] Crossman, E. R. F. W., Seymour, W. D. et al. 'The nature and acquisition of industrial skills.' Final Report on Research Project. Dec. 1957.

[48] Bartlett, F. C. The Mind at Work and Play. George Allen and Unwin Ltd., London 1951, p. 75.

# References

⁴⁹ Heinlein, C. P. 'A new method of studying the rhythmic responses of children together with an evaluation of the method of simple observation.' J.Genet.P. Vol. 36, 1929, pp. 205–27.

⁵⁰ Jones, R. H. 'Physical indices and clinical assessments of the nutrition of schoolchildren.' *Journal of the Royal Statistical Society*, Part I, 1938, pp. 1–34.

⁵¹ Krumbolz, J. D. and Christal, R. E. 'Relative pilot aptitude and success in primary pilot training.' J.Appl.P. Vol. 41, No. 6, 1957, pp. 409–13.

⁵² Howell, M. L. 'Use of force-time graphs for performance analysis in facilitating motor learning.' R.Q. Vol. 27, 1956, pp. 12–22.

⁵³ Miller, R. B. As reported by Annett, J. and Kay, H. in 'Knowledge of results and "skilled performance".' O.P. Vol. 31, No. 2, 1957, p. 75.

⁵⁴ Stroud, J. B. 41st Yearbook of the National Society for the Study of Education. Part II, *The Psychology of Learning*. Edited by Henry, N. B. The University of Chicago Press. Chicago 1942. Chapter 10, 'The Role of Practice in Learning.'

⁵⁵ Gebhard, M. E. 'The effect of success and failure upon the attractiveness of activities as a function of experience, expectation and need.' J.Exp.P. Vol. 38, 1948, pp. 371–88.

⁵⁶ Sullivan, E. B. 'Attitude in relation to learning.' P.M. Vol. 36, No. 3, 1927.

⁵⁷ Hurlock, E. B. 'An evaluation of certain incentives used in school work.' J.Ed.P. Vol. 16, 1925, pp 145–9.

⁵⁸ Sims, V. M. 'Relative influence of two types of motivation on improvement.' J.Ed.P. Vol. 19, 1928, pp. 480–84.

⁵⁹ Johnson, L. W. As reported in *Tests and Measurements in Health and Physical Education* by C. H. McCloy and N. D. Young. Appleton–Century–Crofts, Inc. 1954, pp. 244–5.

## CHAPTER IV

⁶⁰ Travis, R. C. 'Length of the practice period and efficiency in motor learning.' J.Exp.P. Vol. 24, pp. 339–45.

⁶¹ (a) Knapp, C. G. and Dixon, W. R. 'Learning to juggle I.' R.Q. Vol. 21, 1950, pp. 331–6.

(b) Knapp, C. G., Dixon, W. R. and Lazier, M. 'Learning to juggle III' R.Q. Vol. 29, 1958, pp. 32–6.

⁶² Cozens, F. W. 'A comparative study of two methods of teaching classwork in track and field events.' R.Q. Vol. 2, pp. 75–9.

⁶³ Scott, M. G. 'Learning rate of beginning swimmers.' R.Q. Vol. 25, 1954, pp. 91–9.

⁶⁴ Young, O. G. 'Rate of learning in relation to spacing of practice periods in archery and badminton.' R.Q. Vol. 25, 1954, pp.231–43.

⁶⁵ Cameron, W. McD. *Personal Communication.* 28.11.61.

⁶⁶ Lashley, K. S. 'A simple maze: with data on the relation of the distribution of practice to rate of learning.' *Psychobiology*, Vol. 1, 1918, pp. 353–67.

# References

[67] Harmon, J. M. and Miller, A. G. 'Time patterns in motor learning.' R.Q. Vol. 21, 1950, pp. 182–7.

[68] See reference 41.

[69] Winterbottom, W. *Soccer Coaching*. Naldrett Press 1957, p. 204.

[70] Crossman, E. R. F. W. 'A theory of the acquisition of speed-skill' *Ergonomics*, Vol. 2, No. 2, 1959, pp. 153–66.

[71] Welford, A. T. *Symposium on Fatigue*, edited by Floyd, W. F. and Welford, A. T., H. K. Lewis and Co. Ltd., London 1953, Chapter 20, 'The psychologist's problem in measuring fatigue', pp. 183–91.

[72] See reference 33.

[73] Stetson, R. H. and McDill, J. A. 'Mechanism of the different types of movement.' P.M. 145. Vol. 32, No. 3, 1923, pp. 18–40.

[74] Sperry, R. W. 'Action current study in movement co-ordination', J.Gen.P. Vol. 20, 1939, pp. 295–313.

[75] Hartson, L. D. 'Contrasting approaches to the analysis of skilled movements.' J.Gen.P. Vol. 20, 1939, pp. 263–93.

[76] Slater-Hammel, A. T. 'An action current study of contraction-movement relationships in the tennis stroke.' R.Q. Vol. 20, 1949, pp. 424–431.

[77] Fulton, R. E. 'Speed and accuracy in learning a ballistic movement.' R.Q. Vol. 13, 1942, pp. 30–42.

[78] Fulton, R. E. 'Speed and accuracy in learning movements', *Archives of Psychology*', 300, 1945.

[79] Solley, W. H. 'The effects of verbal instruction of speed and accuracy upon the learning of a motor skill.' R.Q. Vol. 23, 1952, pp. 231–40.

[80] Riggs, R. *British Lawn Tennis and Squash*. Vol. 30, May 1960.

[81] See reference 42. pp. 473–4.

[82] Shay, C. T. 'The progressive-part versus the whole method of learning motor skills.' R.Q. Vol. 5, No. 4, 1934, pp. 62–7.

[83] Wickstrom, R. L. 'Comparative study of methodologies for teaching gymnastics and tumbling stunts.' R.Q. Vol. 29, 1958, pp. 109–15.

[84] Knapp, C. G. and Dixon, W. R. 'Learning to juggle II. Study of whole and part methods.' R.Q. Vol. 23, 1952, pp. 398–401.

[85] Niemeyer, R. K. 'Part versus whole methods and massed versus distributed practice in the learning of selected large muscle activities'. Dissertation presented to the Faculty of the Graduate School, Univ. of South Carolina. June 1958. *Microcard* UO–59. 188.

[86] Reported by Niemeyer, R. K.–*vide* reference 85.

[87] Reported by Niemeyer, R. K.–*vide* reference 85.

[88] Cross, T. J. 'A comparison of the whole method, the minor game method and the whole-part method of teaching basket-ball to ninth-grade boys.' R.Q. Vol. 8, No. 4, 1937, pp. 49–54.

[89] See reference 85.

[90] See reference 88.

[91] Rodgers, E. G. 'An experimental investigation of the teaching of team games', *Contributions to Education, Number 680*. New York. Teachers College, Columbia University, 1936.

[92] Poulton, E. C. 'On prediction in skilled movements.' P.B. Vol. 54, No. 6, 1957, pp. 467–78.

[93] Davis, R. C. 'Pattern of muscular action in simple voluntary movement.' J.Exp.P. Vol. 31, 1942, pp. 347–65.

[94] See reference 74.

[95] Bartlett, F. C. 'The measurement of human skill – Part II.' B.M.J. 4511. June 1947, pp. 877–80.

[96] Annett, J. and Kay, H. 'Skilled performance.' O.P. Vol. 30, 1956, pp. 112–17.

[97] Seymour, W. D. 'Experiments on the acquisition of industrial skills.' O.P. Vol. 28, 1954, pp. 77–89.

CHAPTER V

[98] McGraw, M. *Growth: A study of Johnny and Jimmy*. D. Appleton-Century Co., 1935.

[99] Tinbergen, N. *The Study of Instinct*. Clarendon Press. Oxford 1951, p. 132.

[100] See reference 99. P. 132.

[101] Bühler, C. *From Birth to Maturity*. Kegan Paul, Trench, Trubner and Co. Ltd. London 1935.

[102] See reference 98.

[103] Hilgard, J. R. 'Learning and maturation in pre-school children.' J.Genet.P. Vol. 41, 1932, pp. 36–56.

[104] Dusenberry, L. 'Training in ball-throwing by children three to seven.' R.Q. Vol. 23, No. 1, 1952, pp. 9–14.

[105] Gates, A. I. and Taylor, G. A. 'An experimental study of the nature of improvement resulting from practice in a motor function.' J.Ed.P. Vol. 17, 1926, pp. 226–36.

[106] Kinnear, A. D. 'Justice for the young male swimmer.' *The Swimming Times*, Vol. 33, No. 7, 1956, p. 214.

[107] Jones, H. E. *Motor Performance and Growth*. University of California Press, Berkeley and Los Angeles 1949.

[108] Astrand, P. *Experimental Studies of Physical Working Capacity in relation to Sex and Age*. Ejnar Munksgaard. Copenhagen 1952.

[109] Brace, D. K. As reported by McCloy, C.H. *et al. Tests and Measurements in Health and Physical Education* – 3rd edition. Appleton-Century-Crofts. New York, 1954, pp. 85–90.

[110] Dimock, H. S. 'A research in adolescence.' *Child Development*, Vol. 6, 1935, pp. 177–95.

[111] Espenschade, A. 'Motor performance in adolescence.' *Monographs of the Society for Research in Child Development*, Vol. V, Serial No. 24, Number 1, 1940.

[112] Espenschade, A., Dable, R. R. and Schoendube, R. 'Dynamic balance in adolescent boys.' R. Q. Vol. 24, 1953, pp. 270–5.

[113] Tanner, J. M. *Growth at Adolescence*. Blackwell. Oxford 1955, p. 136.

[114] Bliss, J. G. 'A study of progression based on age, sex and individual differences in strength and skill.' *American Physical Education Review*, Vol. 32, 1927, pp. 11–21 and 85–99.

## References

[115] Kulcinski, L. 'Relation of intelligence to the learning of fundamental muscular skills.' R.Q. Vol. 16, 1945, pp. 266–76.

[116] Mirenva, A. N. 'Psychomotor education and the general development of pre-school children. Experiments with twin controls.' J.Genet.P. Vol. 46, 1935, p. 433–53.

[117] Clements, E. M. B. and Pickatt, K. G. 'Stature of Scotsmen aged 18 to 40 years in 1941.' *British Journal of Social Medicine*, Vol. 6, 1952, pp. 245–52.

[118] Galton, F. 'On the Anthropometric Laboratory at the late International Health Exhibition.' *J. Anthropol. Inst.* XIV, pp. 205–18.

[119] See reference 16, p. 4 and p. 284.

[120] Jokl, E. *Alter und Leistung*. Springer. Berlin 1954 as reported in Research Abstracts of R.Q. Vol. 25, p. 492.

[121] Munn, N. L. 'Learning in Children', Chapter 7, in *Manual of Child Psychology*, edited by L. Carmichael. Chapman & Hall Ltd., London 1954.

[122] Henry, F. M. and Nelson, G. A. 'Age-differences and inter-relationships between skill and learning in gross motor performance of ten- and fifteen-year-old- boys.' R.Q. Vol. 27, 1956, pp. 162–75.

[123] Welford, A. T. *Skill and Age : An Experimental Approach*, O.U.P., 1951.

[124] Crossman, E. R. F. W. and Szafran, J. 'Changes with age in the speed of information – intake and discrimination.' Paper presented at the International Gerontological Association Research Committee (European Section) Symposium on Experimental Research on Ageing, Basel, 1956.

[125] See reference 115.

[126] Mead, M. *Sex and Temperament in Three Primitive Societies*. George Routledge and Sons. London 1935.

[127] See reference 113. P. 41.

[128] Hicks, J. A. 'Acquisition of motor skill in young children.' *University of Iowa Studies in Child Welfare*, Vol. IV, No. 5.

[129] Reaney, M. J. 'Correlation between general intelligence and play ability as shown in organized group games.' B.J.P. Vol. 7, 1914–15, p. 226.

[130] Oliver, J. N. *Personal Communication*.

[131] Burley, L. R. and Anderson, R. L. 'Relation of jump and reach measures of power to intelligence scores and athletic performance.' R.Q. Vol. 26, 1955, pp. 28–35.

[132] Johnson, G. B. 'A study in learning to walk the tight wire.' J.Genet.P. Vol. 34, 1927, pp. 118–28.

[133] See reference 15.

[134] See reference 115.

[135] See reference 13.

[136] Woodrow, H. 'The ability to learn.' P.R. Vol. 53, 1946, pp. 147–58.

[137] Wechsler, D. *The Range of Human Capacities*. The Williams and Wilkins Cpy. Baltimore 1952.

[138] See reference 111. P. 43.

[139] Seashore, H. G. 'Some relationships of fine and gross motor abilities.' R.Q. Vol. 13, 1942, pp. 259–74.

## References

140 McCloy, C. H. and Young, N. D. *Tests and Measurements in Health and Physical Education*. Appleton-Century-Crofts Inc., New York 1954. Chapter 2.

141 Highmore, G. 'A factorial analysis of athletic ability.' R.Q. Vol.27, 1956, pp. 1–11.

142 Carlson, H. B. and Carr, H. A. 'Visual and vocal recognition memory.' J.Exp.P. Vol. 23, 1938, pp. 523–30.

143 Kay, B. R. 'Intra-individual differences in sensory channel preference.' J.Appl.P. Vol. 42, No. 3, 1958, pp. 166–7.

144 Munrow, A. D. *Pure and Applied Gymnastics*. Edward Arnold Ltd. London 1955.

145 Karpovitch, P. V. *Physiology of Muscular Activity*. W. B. Saunders Company. London 1959.

146 Steinhaus, A. H. 'Chronic effects of exercise', *Physiological Review* 13. 1933, p. 103.

147 Nunney, D. K. 'Relation of circuit training to swimming.' R.Q. Vol. 31, 1960, pp. 188–98.

148 Scholey, R. *The Swimming Times*. Vol. 38, April 1961, pp. 120–21.

149 See reference 30.

150 Reynolds, S. *Daily Herald*, July 7th, 1961.

151 See reference 69. Pp. 12–13.

CHAPTER VI

152 Swift, E. J. 'Memory of skilful movements.' P.B. Vol. 3, 1906, pp. 185–7.

153 See reference 132.

154 Wolfle, D. See reference 43. P. 1272.

155 Entwisle, D. G. 'Ageing: The effects of previous skill on training.' O.P. Vol. 33, 1959, pp. 238–43.

156 *Observer*, 23.4.61.

157 Munn, N. L. 'Bilateral transfer of training.' J.Exp.P. Vol. 15, 1932, pp. 343–53.

158 *World Sports*, Vol. 22, November 1956.

159 Seymour, W. D. 'Transfer of training in engineering skills.' O.P. Vol. 31, 1957, pp. 243–7.

160 Ungerson, B. 'Engineering psychology; A British Psychological Society symposium.' O.P. Vol. 31, 1957, pp. 215.

161 Oliver, J. N. 'Value of breast stroke land drill in the teaching of swimming.' J. of P.E. Vol. 45, 1953, pp. 49–54.

162 Minaert, W. A. 'Value of dry-ski-ing.' R.Q. Vol. 21, 1950, pp. 47–52.

163 Egstrom, G. H., Logan, G. A. and Wallis, E. L. 'Acquisition of throwing skill involving projectiles of varying weights.' R.Q. Vol. 31, No. 3, 1960, pp. 420–25.

164 See reference 48. P. 141.

165 Welford, A. T. and Szafran, J. 'On the relation between transfer and difficulty of initial task.' Q.J.exp.P. Vol. 2, 1950, pp. 88–94.

166 Gibbs, C. B. 'Transfer of training and skill assumptions in tracking tasks.' Q.J.exp.P. Vol. 3, 1951, p. 99.

# References

[167] Deese, J. *The Psychology of Learning*. McGraw-Hill Book Company, Inc. London 1958.

[168] Holding, D. H. *Transfer of learning between motor tasks of different levels of difficulty*, Ph.D. thesis, Durham University 1960.

[169] See reference 36.

[170] See reference 17.

[171] Thorndike, E. L. 'Mental discipline in high school studies.' J.Ed.P. Vol. 15, 1924, pp. 83-98.

[172] Sutcliffe, A. and Canham, J. W. *Experiments in Homework and Physical Education*. John Murray. London 1937, p. 177.

[173] See reference 144. P. 148.

[174] Morison, R. *Educational Gymnastics for Secondary Schools*. Ruth Morison. 1960, p. 8.

[175] See reference 48. p. 118.

[176] See reference 13.

[177] Siipola, E. M. and Israel, H. E. 'Habit-interference as dependent upon stage of training.' Amer.J.P. Vol. 45, 1933, pp. 205-27.

[178] See reference 174. P. 10.

[179] Witte, F. C. *A Factorial Analysis of Measures of Kinethesis*, unpublished doctoral dissertation, Indiana University, 1953 as reported by V. Wiebe.

[180] Wiebe, V. R. 'A study of tests of kinesthesis.' R.Q. Vol. 25, 1954, p. 222-30.

[181] Scott, M. G. 'Measurement of kinesthesis.' R.Q. Vol. 26, 1955, pp. 324-41.

[182] Laban, R. and Lawrence, F.C. *Effort*. Macdonald and Evans, London 1947, p. 19 and p. 27.

[183] Corlett, H. 'Modern Educational Gymnastics', *Bulletin of Physical Education*, Vol. 5, No. 1, 1960, pp. 11-13.

[184] Schwab, R. S. See reference 71. Chapter 14, 'Motivation in measurements of fatigue', pp. 143-8.

[185] Burnett, I and Pear, T. H. 'Motives in acquiring skill.' B.J.P. Vol. 16, Part 2, 1925, pp. 77-85.

[186] Hall, D. M. Book Review (of 'The Peckham Experiment' by I. Pearce and L. Crocker). R.Q. Vol. 18, 1947, pp. 232-5.

[187] Shann, F. *The Canberra System of School Athletics*. Melbourne University Press, Melbourne 1947.

[188] McCloy, C. H. *The Measurement of Athletic Power*. A. S. Barnes and and Co., New York 1932.

[189] Cozens, F. W., Trieb, M. H., Nielson, N. P. *Physical Education Achievement Scales for Boys in Secondary Schools*. A. S. Barnes & Co., New York 1936.

[190] Mace, C. A. 'The influence of indirect incentives upon the accuracy of skilled movements.' B.J.P. Vol. 22, Part II, 1931, pp. 101-14.

[191] See reference 55.

[192] Cartwright, D. 'The effect of interruption, completion and failure upon the attractiveness of activities.' J.Exp.P. Vol. 31, No. 1, 1942, pp. 1-15.

[193] Allport, G. W. *Personality*. Henry Holt and Co. New York 1937.

[194] Walker, B. *Soccer in the Blood.* Stanley Paul, London 1960.

[195] Elliott, H. *Sunday Times,* 13.11.60.

[196] Elliott, H. *Observer,* 11.9.60.

[197] Commins, W. B. and Fagin, B. *Principles of Educational Psychology.* The Ronald Press Company, New York 1954.

[198] See reference 144. P. 229.


CHAPTER VII

[199] (a) Best C. H. and Taylor, N. B. *The Living Body.* Chapman and Hall Ltd. London 1959.

(b) Winton, F. R. and Bayliss, L. E. *Human Physiology.* Churchill, London, 1959.

(c) Bell, G. H., Davidson, J. N. and Scarborough, H. *Textbook of Physiology and Biochemistry.* Livingstone. London 1959.

[200] *Handbook of Experimental Psychology,* edited by Stevens, S. S., Chapman and Hall, London 1951.

[201] See Reference 200. Chapter 5, 'Motor Systems', by Ruch, T. C., p. 198.

[202] Lissman, H. W. 'Proprioceptors', *Symposia of the Society for Experimental Biology,* No. IV, 1950, p. 34–59

[203] See reference 200. Chapter 31, 'Vestibular Functions', by Wendt, G. R., p. 1204.

[204] See reference 200. Chapter 4, 'Sensory Mechanisms', by Ruch, T. C., p. 132.

[205] See reference 200. Chapter 5, 'Motor Systems', by Ruch, T. C., p. 155.

[206] Weiss, P. 'Self-differentiation of the basic patterns of co-ordination', *Comparative Psychological Monographs,* Vol. 17, No. 4, Serial No. 88, Sept. 1941, pp. 1–96.

[207] Nielsen, J. M. 'Ideational motor plan', *Journal of Nervous and Mental Disease,* Vol. 108, No. 5, Nov. 1948, pp. 361–6.

[208] Young, J. Z. 'The functions of the central nervous system', *New Biology 1,* pp. 54–71.

[209] See reference 16. P. 23.

[210] Welford, A. T., Brown, R. A. and Gabb, J. E. 'Two experiments on fatigue as affecting skilled performance in civilian air crew.' B.J.P.(Gen.). Vol. 40, June 1950, pp. 195–211.

[211] Lashley, K. S. 'Factors limiting recovery after central nervous lesions', *Journal of Nervous and Mental Disease,* Vol. 88, 1938, p. 733.

[212] See reference 200. Chapter 7, 'Mechanisms of Neural Maturation', by Sperry, R.W., p. 270.

[213] Haldane, J. B. S. 'Communication in Biology', pp. 29–43 in *Studies in Communication,* by Ayer, A. J. and others. Martin Secker and Warburg, London 1955.

[214] Vince, M. A. 'The intermittency of control movements and the psychological refractory period.' B.J.P. Vol. 38, pp. 149–57.

# References

[215] Craik, K. J. W. 'Theory of the human operator in control systems : II. Man as an element in a control system.' B.J.P. Vol. 38, pp. 142–8.

[216] Oldfield, R. C. 'The Analysis of Human Skill', *New Biology 13*, pp. 49–60.

[217] Gibbs, C. B. 'Servo principles in sensory organization and the transfer of skill.' A.P.U. 218–54.

[218] Walter, W. Grey. *The Living Brain*. Gerald Duckworth and Co. Ltd. London 1953.

[219] Sluckin, W. *Minds and Machines*. The Whitefriars Press Ltd., London 1954.

[220] Broadbent, D. E. *Perception and Communication*. Pergamon Press, London 1958, p. 297.

[221] Crossman, E. R. F. W. 'The information-capacity of the human motor-system in pursuit tracking.' Q. J. exp. P. Vol. XII, Part 1, 1960.

[222] Meredith, G. P. 'Information and Skill.' Talk on B.B.C. 1958.

CHAPTER VIII

[223] See reference 3.

[224] As reported by Barnett, A. 'The study of the behaviour of mammals', *New Biology V*, pp. 102–3.

[225] Pavlov, I. P. *Conditioned Reflexes*. Trans. by G. V. Anrep, O.U.P. London 1927.

[226] See reference 2. P. 38.

[227] Woodworth, R. S. *Psychology*. Methuen & Co. Ltd. London 1940, pp. 289–90.

[228] See reference 54. Chapter 3, 'Connectionism : Its Origin and Major Features', by Sandiford, P., p. 112.

[229] Thorndike, E. L. *Human Learning*. The Century Co., London 1931, p. 28.

[230] See reference 2. Pp. 40–41.

[231] See reference 2. Pp. 106, 107.

[232] Pear, T. H. *Skill in Work and Play*. Methuen & Co. Ltd., London 1924, p. 31.

[233] See reference 216.

[234] Koffka, K. *The Growth of the Mind*. Translated by Ogden, R. M. Kegan Paul, Trench, Trubner & Co. Ltd., London 1928, pp. 146–7.

[235] See reference 5. P. 243.

[236] Köhler, W, as reported by Koffka, K. *The Growth of the Mind*. Kegan Paul, Trench, Trubner and Co. Ltd. London 1924, pp. 137–41.

[237] Mursell, J. L. *Developmental Teaching*. McGraw Hill, London 1949.

[238] See reference 54. Chapter 5, 'The Field Theory of Learning and its Educational Consequences', by Hartman, G. W., p. 185.

[239] See reference 92.

[240] Bartlett, F. C. 'The measurement of human skill.' B.M.J. No. 4510, June 14, 1947, pp. 835–38.

[241] See reference 92.

[242] Knapp, B. N. 'A note on skill.' O.P. Vol. 35, 1961, pp. 76–8.

²⁴³ See reference 16. Pp. 38–9.

²⁴⁴ Singleton, W. T. See reference 71. Chapter 17, 'Deterioration of performance on a short-term perceptual-motor task', pp. 163–72.

²⁴⁵ Fraser, D. C. *Personal Communication*. 1.11.60.


CHAPTER IX

²⁴⁶ See reference 232. P. 30.

²⁴⁷ See reference 2. Pp. 109–10.

²⁴⁸ Crossman, E. R. F. W. 'Perceptual activity in manual work', *Research*. Vol. 9, No. 2, Feb. 1956, pp. 42–8.

²⁴⁹ See reference 222.

²⁵⁰ Welford, A. T. *Personal Communication*. 23.3.61.

²⁵¹ Gooddy, W. 'Sensation and volition', *Brain* Vol. 72, 1949, pp. 312–39.

²⁵² Hellebrandt, F. A. 'The physiology of motor learning', *Cerebral Palsy Review*, July–August, 1958, pp. 9–14.

²⁵³ Conrad, R. 'The timing of signals in skill.' J.Exp.P. Vol. 51, No. 6, 1956, pp. 365–70.

²⁵⁴ Conrad, R. 'Timing.' O.P. Vol. 29, No. 3, 1955, pp. 173–81.

²⁵⁵ See reference 240.

²⁵⁶ Annett, J. and Kay, H. 'Skilled performance.' O.P. Vol. 30, 1956, pp. 112–17.

²⁵⁷ See reference 95.

²⁵⁸ Lewis, R. E. F. 'Consistency and car driving skills', *British Journal of Industrial Medicine* Vol. 13, 1956, p. 131.


CHAPTER X

²⁵⁹ Abrams, M. *Teenage Consumer Spending in 1959* (Part II). London Press Exchange Ltd., 1961.

²⁶⁰ Nash, J. B. *Children in Focus, 1954*. Yearbook, American Association for Health, Physical Education and Recreation, Chapter 6, 'The Skill-learning Years'.

²⁶¹ Cauter, T. and Downham, J. S. *The Communication of Ideas*. Chatto and Windus, London 1954, p. 80.

²⁶² The Central Advisory Council for Education (England). Ministry of Education, 15 to 18. Vol. II. Surveys H.M.S.O., London 1960.

²⁶³ McCloy, C. H. *Philosophical Bases for Physical Education*. Appleton-Century-Crofts Inc., New York 1940.

²⁶⁴ Heinilä, K. *Leisure and Sports*, publication No. 5 of the Institute of Sociology, University of Helsinki 1959.

²⁶⁵ Hodgkin, R. A. Article in the *Guardian*, Nov. 29th, 1961.

²⁶⁶ Tanner, J. M. *Education and Physical Growth*, U.L.P., London 1961, p. 123.

²⁶⁷ See reference 264.

## TABLES

1. Jones, R. H. 'Physical indices and clinical assessments of the nutrition of schoolchildren', *Journal of the Royal Statistical Society*, Part I, 1938, pp. 1-34.
2. (1) Vandell, R. A., Davis, R. A. and Clugston, H. A. 'Function of mental practice in the acquisition of motor skills.' J.Gen.P. Vol. 29, 1943, pp. 243-50.
   (2) Twining, W. E. 'Mental practice and physical practice in learning a motor skill.' R.Q. Vol. 20, 1949, pp. 432-5.
   (3) Steel, W. L. 'The effect of mental practice in the acquisition of a motor skill.' J. of P.E. Vol. 44, Nov. 1952, pp. 101-8.
   (4) Clark, L. V. 'The effect of mental practice in the development of a certain motor skill.' R.Q. Vol. 31, 1960, pp. 560-9.
3. Shay, C. T. 'The progressive-part versus the whole method of learning motor skills.' R.Q. Vol. 5, No. 4, 1934, pp. 62-7.
4. Jones, H. E. *Motor Performance and Growth.* University of California Press, Berkeley and Los Angeles 1949, p. 37.
5. Seils, L. G. 'The relationship between measures of physical growth and gross motor performance of primary grade school-children.' R.Q. Vol. 22, 1951, pp. 244-60.
6. Glassow, R. B. and Kruse, P. 'Motor performance of girls age 6 to 14 years.' R.Q. Vol. 31, No. 3, 1960, pp. 426-33.
7. (1) Gates, A. I., Jersild, A. T., McConnell, T. R. and Challman, R. C. *Educational Psychology*, 3rd edition, Macmillan Co., New York 1949.
   (2) See reference 111.
   (3) Kane, R. J. and Meredith, H. V. 'Ability in the standing broad jump of elementary school-children, 7, 9 and 11 years of age.' R.Q. Vol. 23, 1952, pp. 198-208.
8. Jokl, E. 'Age and physical ability', *Coaching Newsletter*, July 1957.
9. Lehman, H. C. 'The most proficient years at sports and games.' R.Q. Vol. 9, 1938, pp. 3-19.
10. Sutcliffe, A. and Canham, J. W. *Experiments in Homework and Physical Education.* John Murray, London 1937, p. 173.
11. and 12. The Central Advisory Council for Education (England) Ministry of Education, 15 to 18. Vol. II, Surveys. H.M.S.O., London 1960.

# NAME INDEX

Dable, R. R., 77, 178
Davidson, J. N., 182
Davies, D. R., ix, 18, 19, 20, 21, 93, 174
Davis, R. A., 52, 185
Davis, R. C., 65, 178
Deese, J., 108, 181
Dimock, J. S., 77, 178
Dixon, W. R., 176, 177
Downham, J. S., 168, 184
Dusenberry, L., 73, 178

Egstrom, G. H., 107, 180
Elliott, H., 120, 182
Entwisle, D. G., 105, 180
Espenschade, A., 77, 80, 95, 178

Fagin, B., 122, 182
Falkenburg, R., 31
Fannin, N. C., ix, 9
Fleishman, E. A., 174
Floyd, W. F., 177
Fraser, D. C., 184
French, E., 34, 175
Fulton, R. E., 56, 57, 177

Gabb, J. E., 182
Gagné, R. M., 174
Galton, F., 84, 179
Gates, A. I., 73, 80, 178, 185
Gebhard, M. E., 42, 119, 175
Gibbs, C. B., 107, 137, 180, 183
Gilbreth, F. B., 22, 174
Glassow, R. B., 79, 185
Gooddy, W., 159, 184
Goodenough, F. L., 27, 55, 175
Greaves, J., 1
Griffith, C. R., 23
Grohmann, J., 72
Guthrie, E. R., 4, 33, 144, 146, 158 173, 174

Haigh, A. L., xii
Haldane, J. B. S., 136, 182
Hall, D. M., 118, 186
Harmon, J. M., 177
Harter, N., 11, 14, 15, 174
Hartmann, G. W., 183
Hartson, L. D., 55, 177
Hause, G. W., 61
Haynes, J., 1
Heinilä, K., 184
Heinlein, C. P., 37, 176
Hellebrandt, F. A., 159, 184
Hendrickson, G., 28, 109, 175
Henry, F. M., 87, 179
Henry, N. B., 176
Hicks, J. A., 92, 179
Highmore, G., 95, 96, 180
Hilgard, J. R., 73, 178
Hoad, L., 31
Hodgkin, R. A., 169, 184
Holding, D. H., 108, 181
Howard, P. D., 152
Howell, M. L., 39, 176
Hurlock, E. B., 42, 43, 176

Israel, H. E., 111, 181

Jay, A., 164
Jersild, A. T., 80, 185
Johnson, G. B., 93, 102, 179
Johnson, L. W., 45, 176
Jokl, E., 85, 86, 179, 185
Jones, H. E., 76, 178, 185
Jones, R. H., 38, 176, 185
Judd, C. H., 28, 29, 109, 174

Kane, R. J., 80, 185
Karpovitch, P. V., 99, 180
Kay, B. R., 98, 180
Kay, H., 67, 176, 178, 184
Kimball, E. R., 61

# SUBJECT INDEX

Recovery of motor functions, 135
Redundancy of signals, 66, 138
Reflex actions, 131, 141, 142, 148
  arc, 128
Refractory phase, 127
Repetition, 7, 11, 18, 41, 44, 49,
  100, 143, 146
Reproof, 43
Research, 30, 109, 113
  need for, xii, 25, 68, 167
Respiration, 71, 132
Response, conditioned, 141, 142,
  145
  innate, 71
  learned, 67, 71, 141–7
  similarity of, 110, 111
  stereotyped, 145–7, 151, 153
  variety of, 74, 133
Rest periods; *see* distribution of
  practice
Results, 4–6, 17, 19, 20, 54, 62, 64,
  66, 89, 114, 123, 140, 146, 162
  knowledge of, 32–41, 43, 45, 122,
  167
Retention, 89, 102–4, 135
  and knowledge of principles, 29
Reward, 144; *see also* incentive
Reviewing of a skill, 104
Rhythm, 96, 150
  of a movement, 63
Rhythmic sense, 37, 38
  systems of the body, 132
Rhythms, natural, 116
Riding, 72, 75, 83, 116
  a bicycle, 81, 82, 102, 169
  a tricycle, 71, 73
Ringball, 11, 12
Ring-tossing, 8–10, 27, 51, 52
Rivalry; *see* competition
Rowing, 3, 56
Rugby football, 68, 104, 117, 152,
  164; *see also* football
Rugby footballer, 116, 160

Running, 2, 10, 20, 36, 37, 48, 56,
  71, 78–80, 82–84, 86, 92, 96,
  100, 101, 110, 111, 151, 154,
  161; *see also* athletics

Sailing, 21, 26, 82, 117, 160, 161
Satisfaction; *see* enjoyment
Scrambling, motor-cycle, 82
  of the expert, 147
Selection for coaching and teams,
  39, 98 121
Selector, responsibility of, 98, 121–3
Self-assertion, 116, 117
  competition, 45
  expression, 116, 123, 171
  instruction, 30, 34
  observation, 35
  testing, 34
Sensations, 124, 129, 148, 150, 159
Sensory cues; *see* cues
  events, 124–6, 132
  organs, 1, 5, 64, 84, 88, 89, 115,
  124–9, 131, 132, 151, 152, 154,
  159
  injury to, 5
Servo-mechanism, 136, 137
Sex differences, 42, 43, 77, 78, 80,
  89–91, 99
Shooting, with air-gun, 28
  with pistol, 106
Shot-putt, 2, 3, 31, 48, 50, 51, 61,
  86, 99, 100, 104, 148, 150, 151,
  153, 161
Signals; *see* cues
Significant, meaning of, 18
Similarity of principles, 110, 111
  stimulus, 110–12
  response, 110–12
'Sinker', 75
Size, 74, 77, 97, 166; *see also* build
Skating, 4, 72, 75, 83, 103, 104, 153,
  157